DESPERATE PRETENDERS

Elaine Cantrell

AUTUMN HOUSE® PUBLISHING COMPANY
P.O. Box 1139, Hagerstown, Maryland 21741-1139

The author assumes full responsibility for the accuracy of all
facts and quotations as cited in this book.

This book was
Edited by Gerald Wheeler
Designed by Bill Kirstein
Cover Illustration by John Williams
Type set: Century Schoolbook 11 pt.

PRINTED IN U.S.A.

95 94 93 92 91 90   10 9 8 7 6 5 4 3 2 1

Autumn House Cataloging
Cantrell, Elaine, 1937-
    Desperate pretenders.

    1. Cantrell, Daniel. 2. Cantrell, Elaine, 1937-
3. Youth—Drug use. 4. Co-dependence (Psychology).
I. Title.
        362.293

ISBN 1-878951-04-1

INTRODUCTION

My home became a sick one as drugs caused us to repress feelings, anger to run riot, and family members to become strangers.

I prayed, cried, and ruined much of my health trying to find answers to the drug problem, at the same time syphoning all the joy and happiness from my family. Neither my husband, Ken, Jon, my youngest son, nor I were chemically dependent, but we were as ill as Danny who was "using." Our sickness affected all with whom we came in contact.

Chemical dependency is a disease. It is chronic. In the home of a chemical abuser nothing is normal.

Walk with me through the shadowed corridors of my home. Share my loneliness and frustration as I fought the King of Destruction—drugs—and experience my helplessness and despair as the effects of drugs tore away the foundation of my home. Know my sorrow and defeat as I strove to keep sane in the insane world of a druggie son, a dry-druggie dad, an enabling mom, and an innocent sibling. And most of all, thrill with my joy as I faced reality and found the courage to be me in spite of the attitudes or actions of others.

Each day I know that I am a very special person. No one can take my place. Able to set goals toward unknown limits, I can turn my problems and attitudes toward others over to God as my Higher Power. I don't have to carry my burdens alone.

CONTENTS

C H A P T E R
1

THE GRAY VALLEY

Danny's thin frame bent intently toward the lock as I watched through the glass-paneled door. His face, silhouetted against the dim porch light, wore its usual angry scowl. He cursed as he jabbed the silver blade of the knife again and again into the door frame. Terror stricken, I knew instinctively he had been drinking again. My mind whirled like a car skidding out of control. *If I opened the door, would he use the knife on me or his little brother?*

Retracing my steps into the small bedroom, I fell on my knees. Tears spilled down my cheeks onto the pink bedspread as I prayed while the scraping and jabbing sounds continued. "Oh, God, I truly cannot do it myself. Please protect Jon and me. Please help me to know where to go from here." Suddenly the knife noises stopped.

Jumping up, I ran back into the living room. Through the side window of the small apartment, I saw his shadowy form weaving up the steps of the apartment next door. "Oh, no!" I muffled a scream.

Flinging open the apartment door, I hurried down the steps, running nervous fingers through my curly gray hair. "Danny, Danny, come here. You're at the wrong apartment." Calling softly, I made my way toward him, feeling my long white housecoat catching on the frostbitten grass.

Danny looked up at me just as his knife blade touched the door. Pushing his brown hair away from his eyes, he turned unsteadily and stumbled in my direction. His hazel eyes fluttered into momentary consciousness as he recognized me. Putting my arm around his skinny waist, I helped him walk a jagged line back into our apartment. The stench of alcohol rose from his brown leather jacket. A few steps inside the door, he slumped his 17-year-old body down into the overstuffed brown vinyl chair in the compact living room-dining room combination.

Returning to my bedroom, I lay down on the bed. Still in my housecoat, I felt its edges cold and wet against my ankles, but scarcely noticed. My eyes surveyed the drab walls of the room as an archaic dresser on the opposite wall reflected the street lights outside.

Jon, my 8-year-old son, slept peacefully beside me. His even breathing helped bring my own fast-beating heart back to normal. Gently I smoothed the sun-streaked brown hair from his eyes, then turned toward the wall and cried softly. Lately I cried more than I breathed, it seemed.

* * *

Less than a month had passed since our move from my simple, but cherished home in the country with its three comfortable bedrooms and acres of land. Scenes from the last day at home hurtled through my mind. Events that I had struggled to record in my diary.

The spiral notebook became my only means of honest communication left to me. There I wrote my true feelings, there I expressed my sorrow, and there I found a small amount of solace and relief.

Jan. 13: I went shopping with Lois [an old school friend] today. When I returned home, Ken [my husband] slammed and cussed under his breath for most of the evening. After he came to bed he heard Danny's radio and went and hollered at him to turn it down. Before I knew it,

Ken ran into Danny's room, tearing up the door frame, and threw the radio against the bedroom wall.

Something snapped inside of me. *Everything isn't going to be all right, I told myself. When I wake up in the morning, it won't be OK. How many times must I listen to these fights between Ken and my children? Must I continue to live in this crazy house?*

When my husband returned to the bedroom, I began to attack him as I had for so many years now. "Why do you have to lose your temper with the children? Why can't you ever be kind? Do you think the way you act is helping anything? I can't stand this anymore. The boys need love and understanding, not your mental abuse."

Ken's angry words only added to the tempest over the barren shores of our hopeless marriage. I knew his answers as well as he knew my accusations: "If you'd act more like a wife, this wouldn't happen. Ya think more of that SOB than ya do me. Who're you to tell me how to act, besides I didn't do anything to that—. If you didn't treat 'em like a bunch of babies, they'd act better. When you get everything your way, you're fine, otherwise all I hear is bitching."

Later I wrote in the notebook a diary entry: *I talked to him until 1:00 a.m. and told him I was leaving him and taking the boys. There is no reasoning with him. He says it's all my fault because Danny is in trouble. He won't help me with Danny; he just makes me feel like everything is all my fault and I can't stand it anymore.*

"I'm leaving," I exploded. "I'll not stay another night in this house, not after what you did to Danny tonight." In response, he bolted from the bed, his chiseled face set in rigid lines of anger. His jaw moved as he clenched and unclenched his teeth the way he always did when upset. Bundling into his coat and gloves, he pulled the black knitted cap over his thinning gray hair. Taking his flashlight, he slammed the back door behind him.

As I lay in the bed alone, cold fear kept me wide awake. Every creak or sound of the wind brought a new fear that he might return and kill me and the children before morning.

Returning in an hour, although it had seemed like an eternity, he came quietly to bed.

After 25 years of marriage, I knew I must hold out a bit of hope to him if I was to ever feel safe away from him. At the same time I tried not to contemplate my own needs, much as I might want to. "Ken," I said softly, "I'll be willing to bring Jon over twice a week, if you will leave me and the boys alone. Give me some time to see if our being away from you will help straighten Danny out. I just can't take his drugs and your temper at the same time. It's too much."

Blaming everything on Danny just to satisfy Ken made me feel dishonest. I hated my husband's critical and dictatorial attitude, and I hated him. But the greatest hatred I reserved for myself.

The muscles in his shoulders rippled with raw emotion. I knew his hazel eyes were flashing with anger, although he said nothing as he lay facing the wall. But I didn't expect any response. Sleep brought nightmares of angry voices, packing, and running.

My day began with my Bible and my diary.

Jan. 14: I started packing to leave this morning. First I asked God for guidance to know His will. I opened the Bible to Psalm 107:6: "Then they cried unto the Lord in their trouble, and he delivered them out of their distresses." This gave me courage to go through with it, even though Ken had threatened to kill us, blow up the car, burn the house, close out the bank account, etc.

After stealthily slipping from the bed at 4:30 a.m., I went from room to room like a silent tornado, gathering the various household items and clothes needed. I knew the trailer court, located less than three miles from home, usually had a vacancy sign out. Ken stayed in the bed although I sensed him monitoring my every move.

After Danny's alarm sounded, he entered the kitchen and glanced at the room strewn with sacks of food, boxes of linens, and cooking utensils. "What's going on?" He ran a hand through his tousled brown hair as he jerked a couple of box lids open.

"We're leaving," I said quietly. "Dad isn't up yet, so don't rock the boat. Eat your breakfast, get your shower quickly, and load the car." I had already packed him a suitcase, along with one for Jon and me.

"Ah, Mom, maybe you're makin' too much out of this." His troubled hazel eyes continued to survey all the disorder. "Ya know Dad'll be OK today. Why don't ya just unpack this stuff? I didn't mean to cause all this!"

"We're going. My mind is made up." I closed yet another box, keeping my eyes down so Danny couldn't see my tears. Setting his bowl of hot oatmeal on the table, I returned to the packing.

Jon stared around in amazement when he entered the cluttered kitchen. "What are you doin', Mommy?" He dropped his jeans in front of the wood stove as he bent over his box of toys. Jon's pint-sized form matched Danny's from the top of his brown hair and lean body to his skinny feet, the only difference being the glasses he wore to correct an eye problem.

"We will live in another house for a while, Jon. Don't be frightened, it will be OK." I gave him a reassuring pat and sugared his oatmeal, pushing his ever-slipping glasses up on his freckled nose. *I wish I could give myself a reassuring pat,* I thought, amazed that I could move so quickly after getting such a small amount of sleep.

Taking my cue, the boys went quietly about their routine of school and work preparations. My mind spun like a violent tornado with decisions, plans, and fears. Although my hands shook, I spoke gentle assurances, never telling the boys how grief-stricken I felt about the fight between Danny and their father, how the thought of living away from him panicked me, or the hopelessness and depression that swept over me as I thought about our future as a family. A fierce protectiveness against any more hurt for them and me seized me.

11

Just as we loaded the last of the suitcases into the blue VW Fastback, my heart skipped a beat. Ken opened the back door, his face ashen-gray against his dark-rimmed glasses. Not looking in our direction, he turned his maroon jacket's collar up against the cold and walked stiffly around the corner of the house toward the barn.

Danny wanted out of the car at the crossroads, promising to look for a job and meet me at noon. After dropping Jon off at school, I drove to the printing company where I worked as editor. A smile plastered my face as I entered the shop. Good mornings erupted from my mouth in my usual cheerful voice as if it were any normal working day and I were a normal person.

Standing at the hall telephone, hoping the sound of the press drowned out my conversation to passers-by, I dialed the number of the trailer court. Gail, the wife of the owner, answered. Her voice sounded congenial, but scarcely hid her concern as she consented to have a trailer ready for me at noon.

My marriage, now wrenched apart, received only a short entry in my notebook that evening.

Jan. 14: We moved into a run-down trailer this afternoon. Danny helped me. We are happy. Jon just said, "It's me, you, and Mom, Danny. Guess there won't be any more fussing."

The trailer with its one bedroom (plus a small twin bunkbed across from the bathroom) smelled like roach spray and molded carpet. The small windows wafted cold gray shafts of light across the dark oak walls. The two lamps Gail's husband brought added a "homey" touch to the orange and yellow "Early American" couch and chair, completing the living room. "Just trying to make you more comfortable." Cliff set the lamps on shaky end tables.

All morning dreams of a peaceful time played in my mind. Later, after finishing his fruit salad, Danny slung his jacket over his shoulder and informed me that his friend Paul expected him over at his house.

An uneasy feeling intruded my thoughts. Paul did drugs. Did Danny take them with him? My tired body refused to fight or fuss, so I said nothing of my disgust about his spending the first evening in our new environment away from me and Jon, nor how alarmed I felt about his association with guys involved in drugs.

Jon and I curled up on the sofa to read a few stories before bedtime. Later, lying awake in the thin and lumpy bed, a strange mixture of insecurity and relief swept over me. Finally I allowed myself to free the emotions that I had kept bottled-up inside me throughout the long, tiring day. Hot tears ran down my cheeks.

I longed for my country home and the times when all four of the children were young, their happy voices echoing up and down the valley like tumbleweeds blown by blustery winds. To see them, once more, swinging from the tire swing under the spreading maple on the wide lawn. Would I never know such tranquil peace again?

Danny's knock startled me into reality. The bedside clock read 12:30 a.m. The sweet smell of marijuana radiated from him as he slipped past me to the bunkbed. I locked the door and didn't mention how petrified I felt about his drug use.

We moved three days later when Gail offered the apartment to me. Now helpless and afraid, lying in the dingy apartment bedroom, I suddenly had a strong desire to call Ken. I needed help. How could I manage an alcoholic on my own? How could I get him to stop drinking? Just who did I think I was? God?

Hearing Danny get up from the chair, I turned on the bedside lamp. Slipping my tired feet into my house-shoes and putting on my glasses, I followed him into the kitchen.

"I gotta use the bathroom," he mumbled.

"It's this way, Danny." My hand reached out to turn him around.

"Leave me alone." Jerking away, he continued stumbling around in the kitchen as urine darkened his jeans.

As I returned to my bedroom, his unsteady feet carried him toward his bedroom. His clothes fell in a heap as he crawled under the confines of the blue sheets and comforter.

Tiptoeing into his room minutes later, I picked up his clothes. A small bottle of liquor slipped out of his jacket pocket. With tears of frustration, I poured the contents down the commode.

My sympathy for him was now gone. It was no longer "Poor Danny," mistreated by his father. Instead I felt real fear of him, alienation from him, and a realization that he had a problem I could not solve.

Feb. 13: My mind is made up now. Danny must go to another rehabilitation center. I will call the lawyer the first thing in the morning. I will not spend another night like this one. God help me.

C H A P T E R
2

FADING HOPE

Drugs and alcohol had reoccurred throughout my life like a persistent bad dream. The words "Daddy, Daddy, don't hurt my mommy" echoed from my childhood. I remember my father, wielding a large, sharp knife, chasing my mother. She ran through the living room and into the kitchen where she pushed her way past the white ruffled curtains and through the screened window, fleeing into the night. Then Dad turned toward us three children standing in the doorway of our room. "Get yourselves in the bed," he screamed, voice slurring and face red. Uttering a battery of curse words, he retreated to his room.

My 5-year-old legs felt as shaky as a bowl of gelatin. The house seemed cold and lonely. I ran to the kitchen window and peered into the blackness of the night. Sobs wrenched my body as I called, "Mama, Mama." My brothers, James and Maurice, each put an arm around me, pulling me away from the window and back to the big bedroom we all shared. Three-year-old Rebecca lay asleep in her crib, her thumb stuck tightly in her mouth.

James tucked me into my cot while tears ran down my freckled cheeks. I knew two fathers. One rocked me so lovingly in my little red rocking chair or sang "Rock-a-bye-Baby" to my young sister Rebecca. The other father became a madman when he tasted liquor. I couldn't understand the transformation. My brother James said Daddy drank whiskey. But the word meant nothing to me. I only felt alone and afraid.

* * *

Mom's brown eyes flashed with anger. She held a large brown, oddly-shaped bottle of whiskey in her hand, pouring its contents down the commode. Granddaddy slept soundly in the back bedroom.

His yearly visits brought delight to us children. He could peel an apple, never breaking the continuous spiral of red peeling. "This takes practice," he'd say, as he finished with a flourish, cutting and eating the crisp white slices with toothless relish. And at sometime during his visit, he'd always pull, from his old brown leather billfold, a new dollar bill for each of us children.

My father no longer drank. Shortly after my 6th birthday, he gave his life to the Lord and stayed the kind and gentle man I loved so much. As an 8-year-old, I didn't want to connect Granddaddy with the awful scenes of my early childhood.

* * *

"Mom, Mom, wake up. Dad told us to keep you awake," I cried. Was she dead? Scared at the sight of Mom lying so still, my 10-year-old mind whirled.

When we had arrived home from school, we children had found her lying on her bed. Mom often napped in the afternoon, but when we couldn't arouse her, James ran quickly to get our father from his job at the local orchard. Dad explained that she had taken too many sleeping pills. I didn't understand why we couldn't awaken her. Kneeling by her bed, I put my head on her still hand and cried as her motionless form refused to respond to my pleas. Again a great sense of loneliness crept through me as the ambulance sped my mother away to the hospital.

* * *

As I continued to mature in the rural Christian

community in which we now lived, the memories of drugs slowly faded. When we attended Granddaddy's funeral, I heard Aunt Liz say, "Dad might still be alive if he had left his alcohol alone!"

In high school, I met Ken—older, suave, in the Army—and fell madly in love with him. Once, during our courtship, he came to pick me up from my job as a telephone operator. "Hi ya, Babe," he quipped as he laughingly swaggered up to me.

"Ken, I smell liquor on you!" Tears sprang to my eyes and my heart did a somersault. In anger I shouted at him, "I'll not date a drunk." I never saw him intoxicated again.

As our courtship continued into marriage, Ken frightened me with his temperamental outbursts. Once he slammed the car door on me, knocking my glasses to the sidewalk and breaking them. I knew, with my help, he could overcome it. When happy, he expressed his feelings in loving words, but when unhappy, he showed only anger. We never communicated feelings, values, or plans for our future life together.

"He gets that from his grandpa," Mom Cantrell said over and over whenever she saw Ken's outbursts of anger or his dark, silent moods. "Grandpa never liked to socialize, and he was a moody sort, too."

Years of Army life followed our marriage. Years with liquor as a household word in most homes, though not in ours. I saw battered wives: Sue beaten with an Army belt buckle by her husband in a drunken rage. Swelling closed one of her eyes and a ruptured eardrum caused her much pain. She left her husband soon afterward. My upstairs neighbors fought each weekend, resulting in bruises Monday morning for Alice. I covered my ears with my pillow and cried because of the angry voices I heard in the night. Alice blamed all the loud voices and crashes of falling objects on alcohol. Hating the word and its results, I still felt the pain and fear of a child left alone in the darkness and cold.

We spent three years on the island of Okinawa. Ken had already been stationed there 14 months when we arrived by ship. My husband held out his arms to our son David as he boarded the vessel. The child, barely 2, shied away. From that moment on Ken seemed to reject him, and we began having problems over David's discipline.

During the following weeks my husband wanted to reprimand David for wetting his pants, for making a mess, for wriggling in church. It became a tug-of-war for the three of us. I refused to allow him to punish David if he couldn't show the child any affection. It only intensified his hostility toward his son.

When Ken came home from work, David ran and hid in his room. His sister Anita, barely 6, awoke in the night crying from bad dreams. I fought with Ken over his abusive behavior on a regular basis, many times long into the night. The verbal fights occasionally turned physical, resulting in bruises on my arms and face.

"It's enough. I don't feel like making love when we fight all the time." I ran from the bedroom. "I'll just end it all," I screamed as I opened the medicine cabinet for a razor blade.

Ken caught my wrist. "I'm sorry, honey. I didn't mean to upset you so much. I'll leave you alone. I promise. Just come back to bed."

His moods were as subject to change as a tropical rain shower. When it was up, away we would go for a weekend at the beach, a day at the carnival, or a picnic. Our life resembled an emotional roller-coaster.

My family never learned to cope with his abusive behavior, especially the situation with David. The lack of communication made things even worse. We were a sick family, each accusing the other, never searching ourselves for constructive answers to our many problems.

I became pregnant with Danny just before our return from Okinawa. In my agony, I cried out to God, *No, I must not bring another child into this miserable situation.* Ken felt equally unhappy about the pregnancy. In my desperation I tried lifting my heavy portable sewing machine up and down a stepladder, hoping to induce an abortion, but to no avail.

But when I held Danny in my arms the Saturday morning of his birth in the Sam Houston Hospital, I knew then I wouldn't take a million dollars for him. "You're special," I whispered in his tiny soft ear.

Overseas, then back home, the Army kept us like a ping-pong ball in motion. When Anita reached high school age, I refused to go to Germany with Ken. Through the years of moving I had promised my daughter, "When you reach high school, we will live in one location all four years." Since it was his last tour of duty overseas, he gave in to my wishes.

I searched for a country home for my three children. After several weeks, I found a farm in a small rural community much like the one on which I had grown up. My joy knew no bounds when Ken approved our purchasing the farmhouse with its acres of woods and pastures.

"Now," I anticipated, surveying the old country house, the huge maples, and my contented children, "now I won't ever have anything but happiness. Happiness will be like a sky full of stars, unending. Now my children can grow up like young fillies. They can run this valley and hills. They can have animals, friends, and the security of a permanent home."

The next two years flew on wings of joy as we accumulated cats, dogs, and horses. After 15 years of moving every three years to another Army post, my cup ran over and spilled into the saucer.

Our farm was only 40 miles from Ken's parents, my parents, and my sister Rebecca and her husband, Leo. With their help, we spent happy hours wallpapering, painting, and gardening, the children working beside us.

The maple leaves lay in golden heaps as an old country gentleman came up our dirt driveway one late autumn day. Mr. Briley said he'd owned our farm years before us. He told of felling the logs for the barn and planting the now huge fir tree as a sapling.

When he asked if we owned any chickens and I replied No, he said he'd be happy to sell us a couple dozen.

"Please, Mom?" the boys chorused.

"Only a dollar apiece," Mr. Briley enticed.

Bringing the chickens home in wire cages, we let them loose in the old, fenced henhouse back of the garage. The chickens produced only a few eggs over the next few months. The boys returned time after time from the henhouse in disappointment. We fed the birds the highest grade of feed to encourage them to lay.

When the first dogwoods bloomed in the valley the following spring, Mr. Briley again appeared at my door. "How's them chickens?" he asked.

"Not many eggs," I replied.

"Want me ta take 'em back off yer hands?" His craggy face radiated empathy.

"Gladly!"

Later when I related my experience to other country neighbors, they laughed merrily at my naiveness. We did purchase more chickens, and I did learn that in the winter chickens seldom lay. And I never gave any more chickens free room and board for the winter!

At the end of two years, Ken returned from Germany to begin the last portion of his Army career at a nearby base, returning home each weekend. The chores of caring for a cow, horse, and chickens, and providing wood for the winter were endless. Anita and David—teenagers now —worked during my husband's absence at whatever I asked them to do.

Ken's "Army Sergeant" attitude dominated his deal-ings with the children. "I'm not a robot," Anita said, her brown eyes showing hurt and anger. David asked my help in getting him out of endless chores. He begged me to say Yes when Dad consistently said No.

Danny spoke in a disrespectful manner many times. The two older children used him to express their hurts and irritations to their father. "You ask Dad, he'll do it," David wagered.

"Tell him to quit saying bad words," Anita whispered.

A kind of tug-of-war ensued in our home and continued to grow worse like an insidious cancer. My kinder, more gentle approach and Ken's dictatorial manner struggled violently. He insisted the children hop to attention the moment he spoke. If they didn't, they received a thrashing of violent and abusive language.

Often I threatened to leave, then because of his mental abuse and my fear of him, I stayed.

Ken was always in a good mood when he took us on vacations or a shopping spree. During such times I would convince myself that the other extreme of his mood swings hadn't been so bad after all. Then the roller-coaster would hit bottom and days of cursing and abusive language would follow.

Periodically my tolerance snapped and I exploded by throwing dishes or slamming doors. Many times I ran into the hills where I stayed for hours, leaving my children alone. Ken seemed to take this as his cue to calm down—until the next explosion.

My husband and I seemed to have no common meeting ground. Our family became like a sandwich, with Ken on one side and me on the other, the children in the middle.

I became their go-between with their father and gave them love and support for both Ken and me. At times life felt like a revolving door that never stopped turning.

"Ken, you're too harsh with the kids. Can't you show a little more kindness?"

"OK," he'd retort. "I won't say another word. Ya just wanna' run the show, so do it."

We quarreled in front of the children, many times in bitterly angry words, ending in days of silence between the two of us. I spent all my energy protecting them from his verbal abuse until I felt like a puppet on a string—pulled toward my verbally abused children, then yanked in the opposite direction because of my love for him.

Ken retired from the Army after a year at the local base, and returned home to stay. The adjustments tumbled upon us like an avalanche. My independence had grown each time he took an overseas tour of duty. During them he'd spent much of his time deciphering my letters and deciding what needed "straightening" up when he returned.

Almost immediately I became pregnant. I cried for days knowing I didn't want another child in the unhappy atmosphere of our home. "Why, oh why, God?" I wept bitterly. "I don't need to be pregnant!"

However Jon's birth brought sunshine into our home. He became a welcome diversion from the fighting and contention. The children loved the new baby and rocked and cuddled him like a new puppy. Ken seemed to dote on Jon, barely noticing Danny, who'd been his favorite until then.

David and Danny observed their father's great interest in Jon, how he played with him, bought him toys, but left them out. Yet he had done much the same with the other three children when they were babies, especially doting on Danny.

"Danny, give Jon the car," I would say.

"Oh, yeah, little baby gets everything he wants," Danny would snap back.

Many times when they played together Danny hurt Jon, though he declared it was unintentional.

"Danny, you're the oldest. Behave yourself," I repeated over and over, never asking him why he showed such anger. The pattern happened time and again until I despaired of allowing them to be together.

Christmases brought a reprieve and were especially wonderful with the smell of pungent cedar, sugar cookies, and dressing. The Christmas "spirit" became infectious.

David brought out his blue sleeping bag with the brown flannel duck-printed lining. "This will be all I need tonight, Mom," he said as he nestled close to the tree, the lights reflecting into his brown-rimmed glasses. Danny quickly ran for his sleeping bag.

During Jon's first Christmas, David carried him into the den. The child, with delighted squeals and nearly jumping from his brother's arms, saw the myriads of colors on the tree.

Jon took his first steps the year David began high school. David's first year also brought a two-week suspension for the use of marijuana. When he told me, I felt desperate.

I didn't know what marijuana looked like, or how a person smoked the weed. Utterly humiliated, I felt sorry for myself and for David having to be at home with his father, but I never thought about getting help for him.

Over the next few years, David became less and less interested in his schoolwork and more fascinated with drugs. At the time I didn't know marijuana was a mind-altering substance or that a small amount could have a strong emotional effect. Nor did I understand that his loss of motivation resulted from his increasing dependance on drugs.

When I saw a prescription bottle for Elavil beside his bed one evening, I asked him about it. "Oh, that's a prescription I'm supposed to pick up for Mike's mom," he said. *That's rather odd,* I thought but didn't question him further.

David had always been affectionate. He'd give me a hug each day before leaving for school and one when he returned home. Now Ken chose him as his "whipping block," directing much of his abuse toward David, many times without foundation. And when he did, I'd think, *Why am I so scared?* Then I'd remember how my father shouted when he drank. *Not in my home please, God, not in my home.*

During Christmas vacation David spent hours chopping wood with scarcely time to warm himself by the wood stove. But the boy never received a thank you, hug, or pat on the back from his father for a job well done. Ken unplugged David's electric blanket each winter night and did not allow him to drive the car under any circumstances.

David stood six inches taller than his father by the time he began high school. His stocky build gave him the appearance of a man, though his strength and endurance bespoke a boy. He complacently obeyed his father, seldom talking back to him.

As he grew into a teenager, he began finding homes where a kinder and less pressured atmosphere prevailed. As he began spending more time away from the house, my heart yearned for him. "David, stay home tonight. We'll bake some cookies."

Shaking his head sadly, pulled between his love for me and his fear of his father, he'd decline. "Not tonight, I gotta run over to Fred's." He'd ride his bicycle or walk, if necessary, to get away.

I began noticing other changes taking place in him. One of the evenings he did come home, he fell into bed without supper or my usual hug. "Hi ya, Mom. No supper fa me. Goodnight."

"David, are you drunk?" I asked in unbelief.

"Oh, Brent and I just had a few, don't worry, Mom." And he fell soundly asleep.

Occasionally when he came in and went to his room to bed, I knew he had been drinking. It frightened me. Ken must not learn about it. Although I felt shame for what alcohol could do to David's life, I never considered the fact that he needed help.

During Danny's seventh grade, I returned home from work one night to find David and him sitting at the kitchen table. "You better find out what Danny's been into," David announced. I asked the younger boy for an explanation and then I knew. He tried to talk, but through droopy eyes he only looked at me with a silly grin.

Sending him to his room, I immediately called the

principal. Soon I had pieced the story together. An older guy in high school had given Danny and a friend some barbiturates. They swallowed them without a thought about possible aftereffects. Danny spent the next two weeks suspended from school.

What next? I thought, giving him a good scolding for his use of the barbiturates. "I didn't know what the stuff was. I'll never touch another pill again," he promised.

His use of tobacco started the summer before he began eighth grade. "Danny, you know the tar in cigarettes has many chemicals, including several cancer-causing ones. Your dad has struggled with this habit all his life. You promised me you wouldn't smoke. What's going on with you?"

"Sorry, Mom, I'll try to quit; honest I will."

I spoke to Pastor Ricks, who took a special interest in the boy. In a friendly way, he talked with him about the addiction. Pastor Ricks suspected that there were more drugs than cigarettes in my son's life. He took Danny with him to a local museum, spending all day, and sent him a subscription to an astronomy magazine, trying to spur an interest. We hoped to have him drug-free by his eighth-grade graduation.

The habit still held its insidious grip on him when he stood to give his speech as president of his class. It tarnished my pride in him. Laughter and happy chatter greeted us at the eighth-grade party in the fellowship hall. Danny nudged me shortly after we began drinking the punch and begged to go to a friend's house where he spent a lot of his time. Later we learned he sampled the father's alcohol during his visits.

That summer Danny worked several yard jobs for the neighbors and bought a new 10-speed bicycle. He spent hours riding the country roads. During his jaunts he found remains of cigarettes along the road which he collected and smoked.

After David began staying away from home and Anita left for college 200 miles away, Ken began using

Danny for help with the farm chores. Until then he had allowed the boy to stay indoors where he spent hours drawing and building model airplanes. As a result Danny had little experience with working. This led to a new set of quarrels as Danny's temperament matched Ken's and the confrontations erupted like geysers at the slightest provocation.

Repeatedly, Danny exploded to his dad, "I'm not your slave, and I don't intend to be." Many times the boy cursed his father and showed him disrespect. Rarely did I correct him, believing Ken deserved it.

The summer after Danny graduated from the eighth grade, I talked Ken into taking the four of us on a short vacation. Loving to travel, I felt excited as we drove through the mountains and called Danny and Jon's attention to the beautiful red maples and yellow oaks in the Great Smoky Mountains.

We checked into a motel in Gatlinburg and began a couple days of sight-seeing. While visiting the Indian shops in Cherokee the second afternoon, Danny proudly showed me three $20 bills. "I found these in a billfold on the pavement when we parked. It didn't have any name." When he said he'd thrown the billfold away, I accepted his explanation and suggested he find a police officer and turn the money in. *Strange,* I thought, *he's been with us most of the time. I don't remember seeing any billfold.*

That evening Danny began fussing about sight-seeing on his own. I felt uncomfortable about letting him go by himself, but hated the mistrust I felt. Ken, Jon, and I rode the tram cars. An uneasy feeling blocked out the fun. Jon watched happily as the taffy machine swirled pink and green candy, but I scarcely noticed.

Several hours later we returned to the motel. Danny cursed me when I changed the TV station from a show I considered inappropriate for his little brother to watch.

"What have you been up to while we were gone?" I asked. "Have you been drinking?"

Cursing again, he snapped back, "And just what do ya

think I been drinking?" More angry words followed, with Ken threatening to throw him out of the motel.

I felt a quiver run through me as I remembered seeing my father's anger when he drank. *It can't be, it must not be in my home,* I thought. Later Ken checked his billfold and declared that some of his cash was missing. "Danny, did you take any money from your dad?" I questioned.

Denying it, he stuck to his story about finding the billfold. "Y'all must have just miscounted your money." Then he slammed out of the motel. I ordered him, sulking, back from the swimming pool lounge an hour later.

Years later we learned he had stolen the money. Then, while supposedly sight-seeing, he asked an old man on the street to buy him a bottle of liquor. Danny drank, all alone, while we were touring Gatlinburg.

All that time I never thought about getting help for either Danny or David, refusing to believe that they had a problem. I only knew the anger and contention in our home constantly overshadowed everything. If Ken were only kinder, showed more interest, and related better, I believed, then everything would automatically right itself. Unfortunately, I never realized that Ken had a "problem" beyond my comprehension. One that I could not solve.

At church I always noticed families, especially parents with neat children all in a row usually sitting toward the front. They sat so proper, opening their songbooks and their Bibles at the right time. My heart filled with envy. The fathers seemed so happy, the kids so content. *Why can't I have a family like that? Why must mine be so messed up?*

I never shared the burden of my unhappy home with anyone, not even my parents. Filled with constant shame and disgrace, I considered myself a poor mother to allow this to happen to my kids.

C H A P T E R
3

THE UNHAPPY VALLEY

David, I worry so much about you. Are you staying warm? Do you have enough to eat? Is Aunt Rebecca keeping your clothes washed?"

When the conversation always came around to his returning home, he'd shake his head sadly. "Don't worry, Mom. I don't want you to cry. I'm OK, honest." Then he'd give me a reassuring hug and kiss as we parted.

But I still nursed a great sorrow for David who had moved out of the house. He lived in my sister Rebecca's basement where he existed in a makeshift, cold, and damp bedroom. Often I saw his red Cutlass parked at a picnic pavilion near the printing company where I worked. From that I knew he had been up to see friends for the weekend.

Knowing that he would have spent the night in his car, I usually brought along several sandwiches, apples, and freshly baked cookies or pie. He always received the food with gratitude and a hug.

I erected a fantasy wall of "Well, it wasn't so bad yesterday after all." Deceiving myself about the condition of our home, I excused Ken to David. "You know Dad doesn't mean all those awful words. It will be different if you come back, I know it will. I'll talk to him."

Sometimes I convinced my son and he returned for a

few days, but it never worked. The first time he failed to hang up a towel in the bathroom or to turn out a light, Ken slammed the light out or began mumbling curse words under his breath, and David ran.

Always I made vain excuses for Ken and his actions. Visits to the mall or relatives always began with the children begging me not to have him accompany us. I insisted, "Oh, this time it will be different, you'll see."

As time went on I felt more and more inadequate as a wife, mother, and human being. Ken convinced me that I was the source of the problem in our home. His anger became a manifestation of my own internal inadequacy. After most of our confrontations, he shook his finger in my face, saying, "If you were more of a wife," or "If you were all you claimed to be, everything'd be fine around here."

My low self-esteem prevented me from gaining insight into the problem. I alienated myself from my friends. Many times my reactions became violent— throwing a skillet at Ken, sending dishes crashing to the floor, or hurling a potted plant. Always I allowed him to avoid the consequences of his abnormal behavior.

"Mrs. Cantrell, this is Mr. Brewer. The faculty has voted to suspend Danny for two weeks. He brought liquor to one of the girls at school yesterday. She got drunk and is also suspended."

"Sure, I'll be up to get him." I let the telephone fall back into its cradle. The kitchen's bright yellow counters and red and yellow-accented teapots on the wallpaper seemed to fade into shades of gray.

Danny's freshman year had begun shakily. The tobacco habit still held him in its insidious grip. Mr. Puckett, a supervisor at school, told him, "Danny, the tar and chemical agents in cigarettes will irritate your lungs. You want lung cancer?"

When I got myself under control and had had time to think, I phoned Mr. Brewer and asked him and another faculty member to meet with us as soon as possible.

As we sat together in the sunny office, the men were most sympathetic. I suggested that they allow Danny to move into a more sheltered situation to get him away from the alcohol and tobacco. The school agreed, provided that he stopped smoking. My son readily accepted all the stipulations they set up.

At the end of the two weeks, Danny gave little resistance about the move. "I'll be glad to be away from home, 'specially Dad," he said. My father and I helped him transfer his clothes and bedding.

At the same time Danny took a job at the printing company where I worked. He seldom came into my office, but when he did, he told me he needed toothpaste or shampoo, or asked me to buy him a bag of chips or a six-pack of soda pop. Always I hurried out as quickly as possible to fulfill his every desire, receiving a mumbled "Thanks" in return. I purchased clothes, food, whatever I could think of to make him happy. Sometimes I bought him a plastic airplane model kit or new tools for drawing the war planes he did so well. His eyes and manners told of a war of his own. There seemed to be no way to change his hostile attitude.

One day he sliced a gash in his finger with a razor blade while working on a model. At the emergency room he needed stitches. I learned of it the following day when I noticed the bandage on his finger. "Ah, it's nothin' ta worry about, Mom," he declared, avoiding my sympathy.

Years later we learned Danny not only smoked in his new quarters, but did pot and alcohol. He knew plenty of "guys" who gladly supplied him with the drugs.

While under the influence of marijuana and alcohol one evening, Danny and another student decided to break into the school administration offices. They carefully made their way to the offices where they forced their way through a window. Inside they wandered around trying to find something of value. Finally the other student discovered a secluded closet he knew housed cameras and projector equipment. He banged his way into it.

Not finding anything worth taking, they left. The administration soon learned what they had done and ordered them to fix and pay for all the vandalism.

Shortly before Christmas, I received another phone call from Mr. Brewer. "Danny was caught smoking again. We also suspect he is on drugs. We must expel him for the remainder of this school year." Devastated, I wanted to run to Ken, throw myself in his arms, and sob my heart out over my disappointment. But I didn't because I felt no empathy from him. I felt the blame to be mine.

After Christmas, Danny took the last half of his freshman year by correspondence. I quit my job at the printing company to help him with the lessons. The days were long and boring. Ken insisted our son work for at least half of the day, and tempers flared.

In back of our home grew a large thicket of pine trees where brush had grown to enormous size. Danny, under his father's orders, mowed grass, split wood, and chopped brambles in the thicket.

My son's voice would meet me long before I reached him with the thermos of cool water. He cursed every blackberry vine and bramble that he cut down.

When in a good mood, Ken would allow him to play the radio. Seldom did Danny get to have it on for long, though. His choice of music would cause Ken to unplug it in anger. Then in a few days Danny would beg and receive permission to have it again.

Ken never used tobacco openly. Since his early teenage years he had smoked, but never in the presence of his parents or later around me. When Danny lit up his first cigarette in his presence, a battle of words accentuated with swearing quickly resulted.

"Why can't I smoke? You do!" the boy screamed.

"You won't in my presence." Ken would have forcefully taken the cigarette from him, if his son had not chosen to throw it to the ground. He stomped on it, tossing his head in defiance.

Often I saw puffs of smoke emanating from the pine thicket where he worked. "Danny, why don't you try to quit smoking? It scares me what it's doing to your body!" I thought if he knew how terrible it made me feel, he'd want to stop.

For years I did the same with Ken's tobacco habit. I begged, pleaded, and cried, thinking to touch him by my entreaties. Hoping to cause a change, I tore up cigarette packages and poured water in them.

Once I tried smoking myself, to try to awaken within Ken some sympathy for me having to endure the awful habit. Nothing stopped him. Several times he stopped for a week, two months once, but eventually he always returned to it.

I begged and pleaded with Ken to change, blaming him for the condition of our home. In turn he accused and blamed me, saying the fault belonged in my court.

Always I assumed that if he straightened himself out (or allowed me to) the boys would automatically be OK. Our home would right itself like a puzzle automatically interlocking.

Danny took long hikes by himself. With his first income tax return he bought a 35mm camera at the Post Exchange where we shopped occasionally. His photography showed exceptional talent and artistic ability. He took his orange and white cat, Mittens, and worked with her by the hour. Placing her on a log across the nearby creek, he would encourage her to walk to him, resulting in a beautiful pose. Other times he took close-ups of snow or ice formations. Arranging his model airplanes, complete with human figures, he created realistic photos.

When warm days arrived, Jon, Danny, and I went to the local swimming pool. Danny swam with enjoyment and ease, while Jon splashed in the kiddies' pool. Many weekends we traveled the 200 miles to the college Anita attended. She had found the man of her choice there.

THE UNHAPPY VALLEY

The June wedding had been a wonderful occasion of satin and yellow daisies. The ceremony filled the rustic chapel with beautiful, live orchestra music that she and her new husband Randy had arranged. They made a handsome pair, and as Bernie sang "The Lord's Prayer," I wept my own prayer for my daughter's complete happiness.

Randy's zest for life, his happy and positive outlook, anchored Anita in a beautiful marriage. Just before the wedding she graduated with a degree in secretarial science. Then she worked various secretarial jobs, helping Randy to finish his music major. They lived in a trailer on the college campus, but always made room for us to enjoy their company.

While there I felt like I had been transported to another planet without cursing, arguing, and contention. The love, care, and concern shown me left me revitalized for a few more weeks. Anita and Randy played with Jon as if he were their own. The boy cried each time we left and begged to return.

Many times, rather than deal with Danny's attitude, I left him at home with Ken. Sometimes my mom and dad included him in their plans. Or Ken's parents took him with them for an excursion. Often I felt guilty leaving him behind, but my need for relief from the incessant arguing overruled my guilty conscience.

Danny seemed to enjoy staying alone with Ken. He went to a boyfriend's house, watched TV, or played with his models. My son said his father's attitude was better toward him when they were alone.

As the summer began to wane into fall, I became apprehensive about school for Danny. Would the local school let him back in, or would we have to find him another school? Even he appeared happy, a few weeks later, when I received the telephone call telling me the faculty was willing to give him another chance.

On an amber evening in August, he and I walked once more into the school halls. I checked to make sure that I had his recently completed correspondence school grades in my purse. *Dear God, please let him make it this time,* I silently prayed.

CHAPTER
4

FROM BAD TO WORSE

Hi, Danny." "Great to see you back." Mark and Tom slapped him playfully on the back.

"I can do this by myself, ya know," Danny whispered as he and his friends moved away. I smiled weakly at his retreating blue shirt and followed him as he picked up entrance forms.

"Truman, can I take the photography class?" The teacher nodded and the first smile of the evening spread across my son's face. The man then helped him formulate the rest of his classes.

The school year began in rich shades of autumn. I heard the kitchen door close each morning shortly before time to drive to school. As I scooted into the driver's seat, I always smelled tobacco. "Danny, you know this is against school policy. Haven't you had enough? Don't you know where this will lead?"

"Ah, Mom, ya worry too much. I know how ta take care of myself and that dumb faculty."

"Danny, I can't talk to you anymore. You take a negative attitude about everything. Do you want the faculty to dismiss you from school again?"

"Ya worry too much, Mom," he flung over his shoulder as he jumped from the car and headed toward the high school.

DESPERATE PRETENDERS

The next few weeks brought order and happiness back into our household as we resumed regular school scheduling. In late September, Mr. Wilks, from the printing company where I had previously worked, called and asked me to stop by and talk with him.

He offered me the editorial position at the press. Since my relationship with Ken had deteriorated to a cold war of silence, I welcomed an opportunity away from him and could use the money. I phoned a local kindergarten and they consented to take Jon, even though school had been in session more than a month.

Each morning I drove my sons to their schools, then headed for my new responsibilities. Looking into the rearview mirror to check my hair, I found myself smiling. *Maybe we'll make it this time. Maybe, just maybe it's going to be a good school year.* I felt happiness slowly creeping up my spine. *Maybe I am somebody. Maybe, just maybe I can do something right,* I thought with excited anticipation.

Before the semester ended, I began receiving messages. "You know I feel a lot of concern for Danny," Mrs. Langford's voice came over the telephone in sympathetic tones. "He's making failing grades in English and doesn't seem to care. Tell him all he has to do is ask me about what he doesn't comprehend." The phone rang with similar comments from other teachers over the next few weeks.

October's bright blue weather cascaded over the Tennessee hills when I once more heard Mr. Brewer's voice over the phone. "I'm sorry, Mrs. Cantrell, the faculty has again voted for Danny's dismissal. We are expelling a girl also. She drank liquor your son brought to her last night. Danny's attitude with the teachers is one of disrespect. Most of his grades are failing. Neither of us are benefiting by his being in school here."

"What am I supposed to do? Where can I get help for him?" I screamed and cried into the red telephone.

"I'm sorry, I don't have any answers for you. You

might try another school for him."

Danny's head hung and his foot traced imaginary circles in the gravel. His tan shirt-tail drooped around his jeans, and his jacket and books formed a disheveled pyramid in his arms.

"Well, Danny, what now?" He slumped into the seat like a soggy piece of bread.

"They can have their _____ school. I don't need 'em."

Danny's dismissal hurt, and I felt embarrassed and ashamed. While I knew he needed help, I had no idea where to begin. For hours I cried and blamed myself for the mess my son had made of his life. I found myself retreating more and more into a shell.

Returning home we made a sad pair. Danny slammed his books down on the floor of his room and turned up his radio. I began phoning until I found a boarding school willing to accept him.

"Ken, he must have another chance. If he can just get away from the kids he's been running with, I know he'll straighten out. The boy just needs a different environment."

"He's worthless just like everybody else 'round here. I haven't got money to throw away, ya know!"

"I'll take care of it, don't worry yourself." Wearily I began making plans for work and for the trip. Borrowing my father's truck, Jon, Danny, and I drove the 300 miles to a beautiful, private school nestled among the hills of North Carolina.

The principal's brow creased with lines of concern as he explained school policy to Danny. The boy nodded complacently to the do's and don'ts of dormitory life, classes, and the work program.

He found a part-time job in maintenance, which he liked. A school faculty member told Danny he'd work with him any way he could. My son appeared happy as Jon and I hugged him goodbye. The burden seemed a little lighter as I thanked the Lord for His blessings in allowing my son another opportunity.

Ken's attitude took a 90-degree turn when I returned home. He treated me like a bride. Jon thrived in the happy atmosphere for the next few weeks.

Danny came home by bus for Thanksgiving but spent most of his time out with his old friends. Sunday, I searched his luggage carefully while he showered. Tears rushed to my eyes as I pulled a small plastic bag of marijuana from the folds of his jeans. Tremblingly I hid it in the dirty-clothes hamper.

A few minutes before time to leave for the bus station, Danny exploded like a Fourth-of-July fireworks display. "What did you do with it?" he screamed. His angry, red face stared directly into mine.

"You aren't getting it. You might as well be quiet. Get your things into the car, we need to go."

"No, not without *everything*." He sat defiantly on his bed.

Jon and I headed for the car where we waited. Long moments later he threw his angry body into the car. He gave disinterested "Yeahs," and "Nos" in answer to all attempts at conversation. For the next 45 minutes he sat with his arms crossed, staring out his window.

Tears stung my eyes as we left him at the bus station without a hug or kiss. Jon's eyes were sad as he sat dejectedly in the seat Danny had just vacated. I scarcely noticed as I nursed my own hurt.

The next week I received a call from the boy's dean telling me that the faculty knew Danny hadn't stopped his smoking. They also suspected drugs. "You'll need to come for him," the dean said quietly.

Then he put Danny on the phone. "Mom, I'm sorry. Guess I've messed it up again. The principal and I have talked. I just can't make it in a private school."

Anita and Randy still lived in Chattanooga. I made phone calls, and Randy said he'd be glad to come for his brother-in-law. Danny enrolled in a school near them and moved his belongings into their trailer, staying in a small spare bedroom.

FROM BAD TO WORSE

Things seemed calm as we entered the new year. Danny's schoolwork improved and his attitude appeared a bit happier. Then in February the phone again began ringing. "I can't handle him, Mom," Anita cried. "He's defiant, he's drinking beer and smoking pot in our trailer. I can't stand it. What can I do? The principal says he's having trouble with Danny skipping classes. He suggested a counselor."

Jon and I made several trips to arrange a counselor for this brother and sister, estranged and hurt by the stinking attitudes caused by Danny's use of mind-altering drugs. Danny convinced the counselor his sister and brother-in-law lacked experience in dealing with a teenager.

Finally one evening Anita with broken sobs told me that Danny had run away. She had no idea where he had gone. I was frantic. Believing he might go to David's, I alerted him.

That night I tossed and turned sleeplessly. Ken's snoring angered me. He had seemed as unconcerned as a stone statue about the whereabouts of his son.

I went limp with relief when I heard David's voice over the phone early the next morning. "He's here, Mom, but he doesn't want to talk to you. He wants to stay here.

"Danny nearly burned the barn down next door to me last night. Mr. Simmons almost shot him. Early this morning he saw smoke coming from his barn. When he took his rifle and went out there, he found Danny, along with a small fire he had built to keep himself warm." In the background I could hear his brother telling him to quit telling everything.

"Thanks, David, I'll be down later when I get off work." After hanging up, I sat a long while, crying with relief.

David lived in a small, concrete block three-room house. With the help of my dad and my sister Rebecca, we had provided him with a bed, table, and other necessary furniture. Ken had even consented for him to use an old wood stove to keep the cold of winter away.

The winter darkness had fallen as I drove into David's driveway. Jon went into the house to spend some time with David while Danny walked, reluctantly, out to the car. Slumping down in the seat, he gradually unfolded his story.

He had hitchhiked from Chattanooga with a friend. She dropped him off at a gas station near the airport where he asked if he could leave his duffel bag while he hitchhiked to his brother's. A hippie-type picked him up.

Later I learned that the fellow took Danny to his house and gave him a bag of pot, saying that he could have all he wanted. Returning several hours later he drove Danny to David's house and left him there. Since his brother wasn't at home, Danny took refuge against the cold in the barn.

"I get so tired of 'Nita and Randy's bitchin' at me all the time. I can't make a move they ain't on my back. I don't wanta live there anymore."

"Danny, you've been in three schools this year. I can't afford another one. You've got to stick this out. Will you go back and try?" The tears flowed down my cheeks.

Danny squirmed in the car seat, looking away from me. "Why ya always gotta cry? Yeah, I guess I'll go back in a few days."

"Tomorrow, Danny. I've made arrangements for a ticket for the bus in the morning, OK?"

David agreed to pick up the duffel bag and to get his brother on the bus the next morning. I made the trip back home emotionally exhausted.

Two weeks later Randy called to explain that the principal had dismissed Danny. The boy had skipped too many classes, and the principal suspected him of being either stoned or drunk most of the time. "It's useless for the boy to be in school. What he needs is help with his drug problem." My son-in-law's gentle voice did not subdue the torrent of tears and waves of frustration that rolled over me once more.

FROM BAD TO WORSE

Randy put Danny on the bus for the 300-mile-trip home. A determination to get him an education brought Danny and me to the doors of still another school. I sat with him as the school counselor asked if he would like smoking privileges to which he gave a decisive Yes. I felt ashamed of his choice.

Danny had become a stranger, someone I no longer knew, and certainly one who didn't care for my feelings. Three schools and bad grades left his credits in shambles. The principal and registrar did an excellent job in salvaging enough credits to accommodate his sophomore year.

Each morning I took him to school, then dropped Jon off at kindergarten. Danny continually pestered his younger brother, often causing him to cry. "Ah, you pamper the baby," Danny often snapped as he slammed the VW car door.

Many times as I sorted clothes for washing, I pulled a Visine bottle from Danny's jeans. He didn't wear glasses and had no eye problems. "Ah, my eyes get tired sometimes." He'd retrieve the bottle and stuff it in his pocket.

"Danny, get up. It's time for us to leave for church," I would call dozens of times before he would sullenly drag himself from between the covers.

Ken seldom attended. "Why aren't you going to church today?"

"You get that SOB out of the bed, and I might, otherwise forget it. I'm not leavin' this house with him in it."

When Danny did attend, he sat morosely with his head resting on the forward pew. If I nudged him or asked him to raise his head, I received a murderous look. Many times he'd take the pew nearest the door and bolt for it the moment church dispersed.

I often looked around in Danny's room while he showered. Somehow I felt an uneasy need to search for something I couldn't define. One morning as I walked into his bedroom, I saw a quart-sized zip-lock bag of marijuana lying on his chest of drawers. My stomach churned and my legs went weak. Quickly I went to my room and stuffed it into my purse. Danny didn't mention it until after we dropped Jon off at kindergarten.

"Stop here at the drive-in. I want what ya took from me," he demanded as I eased the car into the Panther Den.

"Danny, you aren't getting the marijuana." Shifting my gaze to the yellow school buses and multi-colors of cars streaming steadily into the school across the road, I sought to avoid the expression of hate that I knew he was giving me.

"Mom, if I don't take this bag ta a guy inside, he'll beat me ta a pulp. Honest! Do ya want me ta get hurt?"

"Danny, get out now. You don't get the bag."

"Mom, I'm serious. I owe this guy some dough. He's expectin' this bag, or I get it."

"OK, Danny, but I better never find any more of this stuff in the house." I shoved it at him, and he bolted from the car.

As I drove toward work I felt completely deflated and utterly dishonest. Later I learned that he had conned me. Owning the marijuana himself, he sold it to other students that day who enjoyed it in the smoking area of the high school.

Danny's English teacher called and asked that he get more sleep. He said he'd been unable to awaken him in class several times. Because of my son's use of drugs, sleep came naturally, even in class.

"Mom, can I buy Tip's motorcycle?" His usual somber face beamed with excitement.

"I don't know. Motorcycles are so dangerous!"

"Aw, Mom. Come on. I could ride to school, and ya wouldn't have ta worry about picking me up."

Within three days I secretly removed several savings bonds from the safety deposit box at the bank and cashed them—the only money we had set aside for his future education—and purchased the motorcycle.

FROM BAD TO WORSE

It was a relief not to have him in the car each morning fussing at me for more spending money or aggravating his little brother.

One morning, several months after he'd gotten the motorcycle, Danny smoked some pot before leaving for school. It made his mind fuzzy, and he barely got over a small bridge before meeting an oncoming car. Veering to the right too far, he hit the gravel on the shoulder of the road.

The cycle flipped into the ditch, totaling it, though he suffered only a few minor lacerations. A friend happened to drive by shortly after the accident. Loading the cycle into his truck, he hauled it back to our house, and took Danny to school.

I had insurance on the cycle. When I received the settlement from the accident, Danny begged for an old '55 Chevy he had had his heart set on for several months. We talked at length about the sanding, painting, and fixing. How he would have something constructive to do. "Just think, Mom, ya won't have ta take me back and forth to school. And I can drive to my new job at the nursing home."

As I took more bonds from the safety deposit box to fully cover the purchase of the Chevy, my mind told me my troubles were only beginning. But my heart hoped that the car would give him a new interest other than drugs.

5

YOU'RE ALL THROUGH, MOM

Do you really think the faculty [of Danny's previous school and much closer to home] will give Danny another chance?" I looked into the handsome face of Mr. Warson. He supervised the nursing home where Danny worked and seemed intensely interested in my son's welfare.

"I certainly do. Danny reminds me of myself at his age. He's had a lot of hard knocks, and I believe if we give the faculty this contract, they will consider allowing him into classes again."

I stared at the document. It read:

Appeal for Danny Cantrell

To: Principal and Faculty

This document attached is part of the application for admission for Danny.

Because of the circumstances of my application, I appeal to the staff of this school to consider my admission.

I agree to comply with the following:

1. I will attend all classes and only because of an excused absence will I miss.

2. I will attend all mandatory student body meetings.

3. I will make an effort to refrain from drinking beer,

but should I fail, it will never be near the school grounds. I haven't used other alcoholic drinks.

4. For personal reasons I have decided to stop smoking. I am still facing the problem. I want to enroll in a stop-smoking program as soon as possible. In the meantime, until I have complete control of the situation, I will never smoke anywhere on the school grounds. Also I will refrain from any outward display of the problem as long as I am a student.

5. I will study and maintain a 2.65 GPA.

6. I will be on campus only to attend classes or organized school functions.

I do hope these conditions will be acceptable to the faculty. These are conditions I will abide by.

Signed: _____

"You mean you actually got Danny to consent to all these things? I scarcely see the boy. He's seldom home except to eat and sometimes sleep. I've tried all summer to get him to quit the drugs. I appreciate what you're trying to do for him."

"No problem. I believe Danny is going to make it this time."

Somehow I managed to smile weakly, not feeling much hope within. I certainly didn't expect the faculty to accept him for the third time.

When Mr. Warson, the principal, phoned the day before registration to say that the faculty had OK'd the contract, I felt like shouting at the top of my lungs.

Danny brightened up. We went together to shop for new school clothes, and he even went to the barber shop for a trim.

The first three weeks of school went like clockwork. He got up when called in the mornings, showered, and drove the old Chevy toward school and work. Tobacco still tainted his breath, however, and the weekends were nightmares. He almost always broke his curfew of 12:00.

Most Saturday nights Danny stumbled to his room in

45

the wee hours of the morning. I always lay awake listening for the car so I could have the door open before Ken awakened.

The middle of September came with a blaze of color. My happiness began to fade as the leaves fell from the trees. By the first of October, Danny spent more nights away from home than he did at home. Questioning brought a volley of cursing. "Why don't ya just mind your own business? I'm goin' to school; what else ya want? Blood?"

He was constantly with his friend Kevin. They had big plans to make money. Danny had asked if he could drop out of school and go to work for the boy's carpenter father. Of course, my answer was No.

My diary recorded my increasing anguish.

Oct. 5: Danny has been gone two nights and one day. Mary, Alma, Mom, Dad, and I fasted for him yesterday. We prayed for him in prayer band last night. God must show me what is standing between me and Him. I just don't feel like my prayers are heard. I have no one but Him to share my burden with, and it is enough. I called Danny at work. He is so hard and cold and unwilling to submit to home rules. Oh God, the work is Yours. I can do nothing. Send the power of Your angels and the sweet Spirit in stronger force today to set him free.

Oct. 6: I saw Danny's car several times yesterday, but I didn't go to him. He doesn't want me now, and I can't help. Doug Wade told me at prayer band that all I can do is show Danny that I love him. I do love you, my son, but your wall is beyond my penetrating. God, please show me how!

The pressure mounted like white-hot lava in the throat of a volcano. While I worked, Danny slipped home for more clothes.

Oct. 9: I talked to Dave Warson. Danny is staying at a friend's. Dave said he didn't think Danny would ever come back home, that my duties as a mother were finished. How much more pain?

YOU'RE ALL THROUGH, MOM

Anita and Randy had moved to North Carolina. Taking Jon, I fled to their house for some needed emotional support and physical rest. As always, they welcomed me with open arms. Randy played ball and table games with Jon. My youngest son's laughter rang like Christmas bells in my ears. Anita's tender regard for me felt like soothing ointment on an open wound. Together we decided that a few days in the Smokies, especially Gatlinburg, offered a needed respite from my heartaches.

An hour before we left, the phone rang. Anita handed it to me. "Hi, Elaine, this is Meryl. Sorry to bother you on your vacation, but Danny has an F in attendance. You know what his contract said. We have heard he is leaving the area with Kevin. I'm truly sorry; we had hoped it could work for him this time."

I collapsed in tears in my daughter's arms. The sobs came like waves on a stormy sea. "Mom, you're just going to have to let him go. He's got to make his own way and his own mistakes," she said.

First I called my father. He promised to leave immediately to find and talk with Danny. "If he needs a place to stay, I'll tell him to come on over."

Then I phoned Ken and asked him to talk to Danny and try to reason with him about going away with Kevin.

After much insistence from Anita and Randy, we continued to the Smokies. There I made several phone calls from the beautiful mountain village. Ken said he had driven up to the nursing home, talked to Danny, and convinced him to promise to wait for me to return.

Oct. 14: I talked to Danny when I got home. He is out of school and will be out of work Friday. He doesn't want any help. Says he will go to Kevin's. I guess it's like Anita said, I have to let him go. God can keep him from going. God help my boy!

Oct. 16: Danny parked his car at the pavilion overnight, just like David used to do. It is more than I can bear to see another one of my children not want anything good out of life. Anita called today to check on me. It is the only comfort I have, knowing she cares. She must be the only one who does.

Oct. 17: Danny came home today, looking for his car title. He said he didn't sleep in his car. Can't get near him mentally or physically. He won't talk about coming home. He smelled so steeped in marijuana, I don't know if he'll even remember being here.

Oct. 18: The police called at 11:00 p.m. Danny was DUI and had stolen someone else's license tags. God seemed to tell me, on the way to the jail, to let the police take Danny to the detention center and not to bring him home. He would never have stayed here anyhow. I pray that the one he stole the tags from will be merciful. It broke my heart to see Danny in such a fix. He cursed me for leaving him in jail. The police officer told me not to listen to him. He hollered at Danny to watch his mouth or, he declared, he would shut it for him. I felt like I was in a bad dream. Maybe he can have time to think it over and see where he's at. While Danny has time, please, Holy Spirit, work for him as never before. Please give him back his heart and his love for Jesus.

When I begged Ken to go with me to the police station, he exploded, "He can rot there for all I care. I'm not goin' out in the cold for nobody!" Although frightened to be out alone so late at night, I didn't want to call my father. I didn't want my parents to know Danny's plight. Shame had kept me from telling them the trouble he had gotten into up to this point, and I couldn't bear to upset them now.

Actually I hadn't shared my heartache and problems with anyone. Often I closed my office door and looked out at the young people playing tennis near the printing plant, or the birds at my feeder nestled among the pine trees, and wished for my life to be as peaceful as the scenes before me. I felt that no one could possibly relate to my problem, that no one understood what I was going through.

Oct. 20: The judge called for me to come get Danny. On

*the way home, Danny talked quite a bit, saying he would
never drink beer or spend another night in jail. We went
and got his car from the local police station. He took off in
it to find his missing tag. Then he came back home last
night. Praise God. Now I leave it up to God. Please help
me not to get in Your way this time, dear God. I want so
much for him to succeed in life.*

*Oct. 21: Dave Warson came by my office yesterday and
made me sick and afraid. He said he grew up in a home
like ours. Said he told Danny he would surely end in jail
if he didn't change. He thinks Danny should join the
armed forces.*

*Ken kept me awake several hours last night as we
fought over Danny living here, Danny's drugs, Danny's
lack of responsibility. He wants to kick him out and I want
to find a solution. His ears can't hear what I say. What
will ever happen to him? I grow more tired and weary
each day and long to find peace. Somehow I must save Jon
with Your help, Lord. Psalm 6:9: "The Lord hath heard
my supplication; the Lord will receive my prayer."*

*Oct. 26: Sgt. Stewart, from the police department,
called last night and said Danny doesn't have to go to trial
today for stealing the tag. I am so thankful. He said the
woman didn't press charges. Danny said he'd lost his tag
somehow and just wanted to borrow one until he could
find his. Then he got stopped by the police for DUI and his
license and tag didn't check out.*

*Danny and Mr. Warson went to Nashville today to see
about joining the Navy. It scares me so. I haven't done well
with Danny and maybe Warson will do better. I don't
want to give him up to the military at 17.*

*Oct. 28: Danny made 83 percent on the entrance test
the Navy recruiting office gave him. He will enlist after his
trial for DUI.*

*Nov. 6: Mr. Warson, Danny, and I went to court.
Danny could have gone to jail for the DUI. Mr. Warson got
it reduced to speeding and no registration by telling them
it hurt his chances of getting into the Navy. I hope Danny*

lives long enough to be grateful.

Danny, Ken, and I sat in our living room entertaining two sharp-looking men from the Navy Recruiting Service in Nashville. One of them asked us if we were willing to allow our 17-year-old son to join the Navy and if we were willing to sign to that effect.

Ken sat with a scowl on his face, saying little. I felt uncomfortable. Danny acted as if he didn't realize the seriousness of the situation. The men set his induction date for August of the following year.

The spiral notebook became more and more my only solace. I wrote in it thoughts that I longed to express to Ken but couldn't.

Nov. 12: I called a hotline in Atlanta for information on drugs. Somehow I had an excited feeling that maybe it was the beginning of something new. I stood by the fridge and cried out to God afterward, "If You will save my son from this awful thing, I will dedicate my life to helping others." And I mean it. The hotline is organizing a parent's phone-robin, and I'm going to help in it. Danny didn't come in until midnight, and I've decided to take the car away for a week. Ken got angry because Danny got angry. It's all so hopeless.

Nov. 15: Danny stayed out until 1:00 a.m. Friday night. When I told him he couldn't drive his car, he took off in it Saturday afternoon and hasn't been back since. Yesterday morning I called the police to ask them to find him, but they didn't. I saw his car up at the pavilion last night, so he is OK. The pain I feel for him is nearly more than I can bear.

Nov. 16: Danny got a job today at a meat-packing factory. He goes to work at 5:00 p.m. At least five nights a week I will have peace knowing where he is. And he has come back home to sleep. I had to buy him rubber boots to work in. The Lord is so good to him now. He will save Danny from himself and also take some of the worry from my shoulders.

Two weeks later, Danny's announcement of being "let

go" from his job shadowed our Thanksgiving celebration. Actually it came as no surprise as I had had several phone calls asking his whereabouts when he should have been at work.

Nov. 28: Danny drank every night after he got his severance pay. Now he has been gone two nights. I'm going to take his car keys and see if this may help. Otherwise I fear he will surely hurt someone eventually. God will have to protect me as I do this because I don't know how angry this might make him. Isaiah 41:10: "Fear thou not for I am with thee."

As I made preparations for Christmas, Danny continued to drink. My sense of helplessness left me physically ill. Although I continued to work, I spent more time with the door to my office closed, crying and pleading with God to show me what to do. At night I slept in Danny's bed to avoid the endless arguments with my husband: me insisting that he display more concern for Danny, and Ken retorting that if I showed him more care, Danny wouldn't have a problem.

Dec. 1: Danny has been gone every night except one since he got paid. I've written him a hard letter, trying to reach him and tell him that he can't stay away from home anymore. God help that I said the right thing—if not, make it right when he reads it. This is such a miserable life, I need Your help, Lord! I don't have anyone to help me.

Dec. 2: Well, I didn't need to write the letter. I had to go and tear it up. The police got Danny for DUI, possession of marijuana, and leaving the scene of an accident. Thank God, he only tore up a man's mailbox and yard. The police found a whole bag of marijuana in the car. The juvenile judge is so sympathetic and wants a drug clinic for Danny. The regular judge I talked to first had said that Danny was going to a reform school. Oh God, if only it will not be too late to help him. I asked the juvenile judge about the Navy. He said it probably blew his chances since

51

this was more than the limit of 1/2 ounce allowed for enlistment.

Danny, drunk, had left his girlfriend at her house, had had a blackout (he was conscious, but later would not remember anything), then ran over a man's mailbox and into the man's yard. Before coming to a stop, he had approached to within a foot of hitting the bedroom window near where the man's daughter lay sleeping.

The judge suggested that if I could get Danny into a rehabilitation unit before his trial, the sentencing might be lighter. He gave me the name of one of the men who worked at a rehab in a hospital near where my sister, Rebecca, lived.

I made the arrangements to admit Danny to the drug rehab the following Friday, though I left him at the detention center. Knowing that I had emotionally reached the breaking point, I did not visit him but sent clothes by my father for him.

Though I found it extremely difficult to tell Dad the trouble Danny had made for himself, I welcomed his sympathetic arms. The sympathy was more than I had received from Ken, who had retreated from me more and more.

CHAPTER
6

THE GREAT PRETENDER

Driving the 40 miles to Madison, I shook the door of the Navy recruiting office at 8:00 a.m. That day would prove to be one of the longest and most exhausting yet in my struggle to find help for Danny.

The Naval recruiters had taken his birth certificate when they interviewed us and had not returned it yet. His Army ID card had expired and I needed it for insurance. A prerequisite for such a card was a birth certificate, so our day would include the 110 mile trip to the nearest Army Post for another ID.

Nearly half an hour later, a Naval officer drove up beside me and explained that the office had moved around the corner. Within minutes I headed for the county courthouse. I had not seen Danny for three days. After the jailer unlocked the iron-barred door, I walked into the small iron-barred cubicle. The man locked the door behind us, then went through another iron-barred door and past several cells until he stuck his key into one of the cell-door locks.

A disheveled, barefoot son came out of the cell and accompanied the officer into the cubicle where I waited. We hugged as he sat down beside me on the cold bench.

Late that "terrible day" I recorded its events in my diary.

Dec. 5: Danny cried as I told him that he had to choose between boys' school or the Care Unit at the local hospital. He agreed to go to the Care Unit. The jailer let us out and we started for the Army Post. He cried and angrily banged on the car until we almost reached home where he calmed down a little and asked to phone a girl. Then we headed on our way. When he asked to drive, I let him.

Danny said he got eggs and a sausage and biscuit or two little pancakes and a sausage with a tin cup of coffee for breakfast, beans and corn for dinner, and two sandwiches for supper while in jail, and that none of it tasted good.

He had cried all the first day in jail because he couldn't remember why the police had brought him there. The second day he got hold of a book to read, then Papa [my father] brought him clothes and a note from me saying I'd be there the next day, and he felt better.

We obtained the ID card all right and headed toward the Care Unit at the hospital. When Danny realized we weren't going back home first, he got very angry. He asked for just one more night out. As I drove, he jerked the steering wheel and I thought we'd wreck. I talked real sternly to him, and we continued on to the hospital with him begging all the way to go home one more night.

As we checked him in at admitting, he made quite a scene. Then the heavyset nurse came down to get us. Danny said he hated me, that he didn't think they'd ever let him go, that he wished he'd died in his car.

A social worker and the nurse talked to us, getting needed information for the records. Danny still wanted to go home. Finally the nurse asked me to leave the room. She came out in a few minutes and told me to just go, that he'd be OK.

I shook and cried as I left but I knew he'd be safe and on the road to recovery.

I went by and told David and then brought my exhausted self home.

As I made my daily visits, Danny wanted me to get

coffee and cigarettes for him. Other than wearing the required hospital greens until he earned points enough to get back into his jeans, nothing seemed any different with him.

Buying him a car model with a set of model paints, I set up a small Christmas tree in his room. It strained my already limited Christmas budget. Later I brought him homemade Christmas candy and cookies. Nothing impressed him enough to say "Thanks." I came away each time feeling hurt and confused.

Dec. 8: The judge took Danny's license for three months and put him on probation based on how he does at the Care Unit. We were the second ones called, so we didn't have to wait long. Had to pay $70 for DUI and court cost and $100 to the man whose yard he had torn up. Danny called this girl he likes, then we went right back to the Care Unit. He didn't offer any resistance about returning or about not driving. If God hadn't impressed the judge to tell me about the Care Unit, Danny might be at a penal farm today. Psalm 50:15: "Call upon me in the day of trouble; I will deliver thee, and thou shalt glorify me."

I kept Ken informed about our son, encouraging him to go with me each time I went to visit. Finally the night arrived for the family conference that was part of his therapy program. After much begging and pleading on my part, my husband consented to accompany me.

Dec. 10: We went down last night for the family counseling. Danny really reacted to Ken being there. They barely spoke. I'll have to find out if he should come. Ken acted miserable. What will ever happen to us, Lord?

Dec. 15: Saw Danny Sunday and left him unhappy as we had to decide on who would be allowed to visit him. He acts so standoffish, and yet I can see he is so lonely. David took him some cigarettes, something I can't force myself to do. Saw Danny yesterday, and he seemed more calm. He hugged me back. I've tried talking to Ken about how he needs to relate to Danny. Nothing I say seems to penetrate him.

Dec. 16: Danny put in for a six-hour pass. They said No because they want him to open up and get all the hostilities and problems aired out. They say Danny is just coasting so he can get out. He's being GOOD but not allowing anyone to break down his wall of denial. Probably he'll be angry with me for not bailing him out.

As Christmas approached, a mixture of fear and happiness stirred within me. Anita and Randy planned to visit Christmas weekend. I hoped Danny could be home for a few hours.

God always provided just enough money for me to get by. I received a $100 bonus at work, which added to my Christmas gift giving. Ken allotted me a certain amount and no more. Thus I had to scrimp and save most of the year to buy expensive presents for everyone.

I hoped in this way to bring some material happiness even if we couldn't experience the heartfelt happiness I always hoped and dreamed of.

When I baked Christmas sugar cookies, Jon helped me decorate them with colored sugar. We sang Christmas carols as we traveled to school each morning and wrapped presents with bright red and green paper. I set up the cedar tree that Ken had cut for me beside the fireplace in the living room. Jon and I spent several happy hours hanging blinking lights, glittering balls, and silver tinsel. Everything looked nice. The excitement of the season brushed sadness from my heart like a feather duster.

Danny seemed to think that he could receive a weekend pass for the holidays. I spoke with the director who replied, "If Danny continues to cooperate, I see no problem with him returning home for a short weekend."

Dec. 21: Saw Danny Sunday. He became angry and refused to understand why he couldn't drive the car when he comes home for the holidays, even though he has no license. It's as if he can't or won't understand right and wrong.

The staff put his roommate back in greens for getting

angry. They suspected drugs, but Danny said the test proved negative. The psycho ward came and took him and locked him up until he put his greens back on. Sounded frightening to me.

Danny's roommate said he'd been at the penal farm. He told him the inmates there put a pillowcase over his head the first night and beat him until the pillowcase became bloody. Danny said he sure wouldn't want to be there.

Dec. 23: Today when I went to see Danny we wound up arguing again about the car. Charles, the director, had us go into a conference room where we talked awhile. Helps to have someone to help me.

No one had ever participated with Danny and me in a discussion before. It felt good to know that I had some sense. My son often called me crazy, and sometimes I thought I might be.

Afterward I hurried home to greet Anita and Randy. The cold and rainy day made the house seem warm and cozy. It blazed with Christmas lights and the colors of brightly-colored wrapping paper, and the aroma of the cookies, stollens, and cakes I had been busily baking late into the evenings for several weeks scented the air. Ken made himself scarce as usual, and the rest of us chatted happily until late in the evening.

Christmas Eve Randy volunteered to go the 40 miles to pick up his brother-in-law at the rehab center, an offer I gratefully accepted. Danny had agreed to stop for a much-needed haircut on the way home.

Anita and I busied ourselves with cooking for Christmas Day and fixing supper for their return. For weeks I had begged Ken to go to his sister's for Christmas Day so I could invite all of my family to be with me. He finally consented.

When I welcomed Danny with open arms, he smiled and seemed genuinely happy to be with us. He even carried on a conversation with Anita and Randy.

Early in the afternoon David arrived. We ate the

Christmas supper of ambrosia, toasted cheese sandwiches, and Christmas sweets. The fireplace glowed and Ken began giving presents to Jon for distribution.

David liked the tan sweater with the suede accents. He also enjoyed the $20 bills I had placed in each pocket. Anita and Randy raved about their sweaters, while Ken seemed pleased with his warmly padded maroon jacket. Danny opened his gift to find a note to ask me about it.

I steered him to Jon's bedroom closet and placed a brown Air Force-style leather jacket in his hands. His smile spreading from ear to ear, he hugged me and tried it on. A perfect fit.

Jon busied himself playing with his new truck and semitrailer as we began picking up wrapping paper, ribbons, and bows. David made an early exit and Ken vanished outdoors where he spent a lot of time when the children were around. We settled down to an evening by the fire with the stereo playing the wonderful Christmas carols.

"Mom, I want the car keys. I'm only going over to Patty's. I'll just go there, call ya to let ya know I'm there, stay awhile, and come right back. I just need ta get out awhile."

"No, Danny. You know the court order. No license, no driving. And besides, the leave is only for home, nothing else."

"Ah, come on, Mom, ya know I've been stuck in that _____ hospital for two weeks. Give me a break."

"No keys, Danny."

The badgering got heavier with him calling me abusive and disrespectful names. When I went from room to room to get away from him, he followed me. Finally I could stand it no longer and locked myself in the bathroom.

He stood outside, hollering and banging on the door. Anita finally told him that if he didn't leave, she'd have Randy forcefully remove him.

At that point he went outside and sat in his car until

far into the night. His abuse left me physically and mentally exhausted. Collapsing into the bed, I did not care if he ever came inside again.

With Ken gone on Saturday, we loosened up and everyone seemed to have a wonderful time together. Rebecca and Leo came with their sons as did my mother and father. We sang Christmas carols and enjoyed a scrumptious Christmas dinner.

Danny's melancholy mood changed to defiance as the afternoon lengthened. He began the car key scenario again. When I threatened to take him back to the rehab early if he didn't hush, he slammed out of the house and headed down the road, the icy rain blending the sheen of the jacket with that of his brown hair.

I glanced anxiously out of the window as the afternoon turned into shades of evening. At dusk I saw him slide into the driver's seat of his Chevy, and he stayed there. The rest of the family exchanged more gifts and played a game of trading small, inexpensive presents.

My only entry in my diary, on what should have been a wonderful Christmas, read:

Dec. 25: David took Danny back at 5:00. He didn't even tell us goodbye and shook his finger in my face, telling me to bring the keys to him at the rehab.

Dec. 29: Ken and I had a conference with Danny's counselor. He told us that our son had gotten a can of beer Saturday night on his way back. The rehab counselors thought it best to drop him back a level. Danny called the Navy recruiter and told him about being in the rehab for drugs and DUI, so we don't know if he's still in the Navy. The counselor encouraged us to go to the Alcoholic Anonymous meetings. Danny seemed in a pretty good mood though Ken didn't say much to him. I don't know how any of this can ever work. Danny says he wants to go back to school.

The next day I received a document in the mail. Opening it, I read:

30 DEC 82: Discharged this date by reason of Convenience of the Government.
Authority: CruitmanENL, Chapter 7 and Milpersman 3850300.2e (13).
REASON: Moral disqualification.
Not recommended for reenlistment. Reenlistment may not be effected without the prior approval of the Navy Recruiting District Commanding Officer (non-prior service personnel) or the Commander Naval Military Personnel Command (prior service personnel).
Signed: R. K. Farver
CDR USN/Commanding Officer

I felt a mixture of both shame and joy, never having wanted him in the Navy in the first place.

Jan. 2: Danny is out of the Navy. God's will be done for him. He is back to level two because of the beer and for an emergency light going off in his room. He no longer has Jeff for a roommate. We talked some about going to look over the Bridge, which is like a half-way house where they rehabilitate guys. He doesn't want to go. I encouraged him to make some kind of plan for himself. He has in mind living with David, but his brother can't handle him, and David knows it. Isaiah 49:23: "I will contend with him that contendeth with thee, and I will save thy children."

Jan. 4: Danny called last night to tell us that he wants to get out, although he really doesn't have any idea what he wants to do. He's still choosing a lonely path for himself.

Jan. 6: Our insurance covers only 21 days, so we are supposed to talk to the doctors about Danny getting out. God will work with us and give us wisdom, I know. Isaiah 41:10: "Fear thou not, for I am with thee; be not dismayed for I am thy God. I will strengthen thee; yea, I will help thee; yea, I will uphold thee with the right hand of my righteousness."

Jan. 7: I brought Danny home. He and I talked to the doctors before leaving. They said the major problem is

Ken. Danny has to learn to give in, if Ken won't. I feel so depressed about it all, and am hoping the Bridge can help.

The next day I finally arranged an appointment with Mrs. Cannon, who, with her husband, kept eight to ten young men in their rambling ranch-type home to rehabilitate them from drugs, get them jobs, and give them direction in a drug-free lifestyle.

Jan. 8: Mrs. Cannon, from the Bridge, came to talk to me. I've tried to contact her for a week. She said they don't take individuals as young as Danny. I felt a sense of horror as she told me with tears that it would take 30 days for his system to eliminate the marijuana in it. She advised me to send him to STRAIGHT, a program in Ohio and Atlanta. I tried calling them yesterday, but never got the right person. It will mean more money. This past bill from the hospital will be over $4,000 after the insurance pays its part. But how can I not do it?

After much phoning I did reach a Straight staff member who promptly sent me materials about the program. I left them lying in a prominent place on the coffee table, hoping Danny would read them.

Jan. 20: Danny refused to go to church and made an ugly scene, saying, "I never wanted to come back to this Godforsaken hole," plus a lot of other stuff. Ken stayed home while Jon and I went to church. Danny walked off before I got home, and I didn't hear from him until 11:00 p.m.

Sunday Danny acted better, worked a lot on his model car, then because he put the pieces he'd painted to dry by the stove, Ken got angry and they ended up exchanging a battery of words. When I talked to Danny later, he said it never works, that he always messes everything up.

Jan. 12: We went back to the judge yesterday. He is putting Danny in the aftercare program at the hospital and is sending him to see a psychiatrist, Tom Suren. The whole family will have to go with him. I pray to God that Ken will cooperate in all this. He needs it as much as Danny.

Jan. 13: I wrote a note to Ken about Danny's situation, and he isn't standing in our way, although he says he won't go to the psychiatrist. I hope the psychiatrist will be able to help Danny.

CHAPTER
7

AMAZING GRACE

Before we made our first visit to the psychiatrist, I separated from my husband and moved into the trailer court near my work.

The spiral notebook became even more my friend and confidant. My entry on January 29 read: *It is two weeks today since we left Ken. Jon speaks little of his father. He and I go over to see him on Sunday and Tuesday nights for an hour. My feelings are very confused. I want to move again because I'm sure Danny is doing drugs at a neighbor's house. He drank one night after we moved here to the apartment, but hasn't done so again.*

Danny started back to school on the 19th. The judge told him on the 18th that he could drive to school and to aftercare. Nothing else until March.

Ken has been very kind, of course, now that we're away. God has led me this far, and I know He isn't going to forsake me now. I must not move without knowing it is from God. Until now I never thought I could get away from Ken. May God never let me forget what I've been through. Lead me, Lord. Thy will be done in each of our lives.

Only my supervisor at work knew of my separation from my husband. I sat with Ken at church so as not to arouse undue questions since I had enough problems with Danny without having to go into detail with every-one regarding my separation.

My life had so completely centered around Danny that it had caused me to lose sight of myself and my marriage. I no longer knew who I was, what I wanted from life, or what my capabilities were. My son had become my life.

When I worked, Danny consumed my thoughts, draining me of physical and mental energy. "You know, I've been thinking we should start a prayer band here at work for one another. I'm sure all of us have our trials," Leila spoke softly as she stood near my desk. I felt her concern and suspected she must know of my separation.

"Oh? What a nice thought." I passed her remark off, quickly changing the subject. I certainly didn't intend to share any of my problems in a prayer band with women who had "perfect" sons, homes, and marriages!

Jan. 30: David came over for dinner today. I suggested we all go for a ride in Danny's Chevy after dinner. We went to the post office, then for a drive. It was raining and the car wipers didn't work. We laughed and had such a good time. I loved being with the boys.

After we went down to Rebecca's tonight, Danny left for a couple of hours and then came in to bed. Lord, help me to find every way to make home so pleasant that he won't want to go elsewhere.

"Mrs. Cantrell, this is Tom Suren [he was the psy-chologist the court had referred us to]. The judge just called to inform me Danny is being held in jail again for DUI and possession of marijuana."

I was at work and had just finished lunch. The glow of the weekend ride still lingered in my heart. For a change my Monday had seemed bright with promise that Danny might be actually breaking free from his destructive pattern, that our home might be settling down to a normal one.

Quickly grabbing my coat, I told Leila that I felt ill and needed to go home. Tears blinded my eyes as I drove the half mile to the apartment. Slamming the door behind me, I headed for the telephone again. "Judge Gray, this is Mrs. Cantrell. What do I do now?"

"Mrs. Cantrell, there is only one thing you can do. Before Danny's trial, you must find a rehabilitation center for him. It's that or reform school. He cannot continue to be a menace to society."

The next few days were a maze of frustrated tears and phone calls as I left my son sitting in the confines of the county jail.

Feb. 2: I went and got Danny today. He cried on the way home and said he could never stand to be in jail, that he had stayed in a cell all by himself. He couldn't believe the judge had let him out. The judge had said for him to get a lawyer and that he would go to reform school.

Danny said that he wants help and wanted me to ask if he could go to Straight. The judge has given me the phone number for a man in Nashville to talk about a charismatic place in Chattanooga to send Danny. We have an appointment Friday. Danny asked me if I felt disappointed. He said he couldn't believe how he always got caught.

Later that evening I took Jon's birthday cake to Ken. My parents and his parents ate cake and ice cream with us to celebrate Jon's 6th birthday. Snow began falling as the boy and I returned to the apartment.

I didn't mention to my husband or either set of parents anything about what had happened. Instead I still kept all the pain buried deep within my heart.

Feb. 5: Charlie, at the Nashville center, seemed very nice. He spent an hour talking to Danny. The Pentecostal and Nazarenes offer the program. It's a charismatic group, and they won't accept anyone who doesn't want Christ to be first in their lives.

Charlie said Danny didn't show any interest in Christianity and therefore they couldn't accept him. While he and Danny talked in his office, I sat in the waiting room reading the brochure about the place and about how

*young people were accepting Christ there. I cried and
fantasized about Danny being one of those Christ-filled
young people.*

*I thought I'd fall apart when Charlie said they couldn't
accept Danny. Frantically I tried to get control of myself as
Danny and I walked silently back to the car.*

*We talked a lot on the way home. Danny wants me to
tell the judge to keep his license. He wants to stay home
and behave. Unfortunately I have mixed feelings about it
all. I doubt that he will quit the pot, especially since he
admits to still using it. He has an appointment to go see
Tom [Suren] tomorrow. Together maybe we can figure
something out.*

*We stopped by the mall to buy Danny some tennis
shoes, and I called a ranch for boys. They wanted $500 a
month for him to stay there. There isn't any way we can do
that. Dear God, help me. Help Danny find the way to
become a useful person to society once more. Don't let him
destroy the fine brain You've given him!*

*Feb. 8: Tom [Suren] told Danny it was time he made
some decisions, but didn't do a thing else. Danny became
very morose and worried. I had to go and tell Ken about
all the mess we're in. I had a hard time talking him into
going with us to court, but the judge said he should be
there. It will be his first time to attend with us.*

Ken and I stiffly approached the tall brown oak
bench. Danny stood between us, wearing his dark blue
suit. His black cowboy boots covered with mud made a
sad picture.

*Feb. 9: We sat from 9:00-11:15 before the judge finally
called us. Right off, he told us that we needed to hire an
attorney. Ken requested a public defender. The judge
angrily told him the case didn't warrant it.*

*A lawyer took us to the judge's offices, asking Danny
questions and ignoring Ken and me. We have three weeks
before we appear before the judge again. The judge
commented that if Danny was guilty as charged, he would
send him to the State Department of Corrections. The*

lawyer charged us $250, which nearly killed Ken. I'll pay it all back, God help me. Jeremiah 31:17: "And there is hope in thine end, saith the Lord, that thy children shall come again to their own border."

While I waited for the lawyer to work a miracle for my son, Danny lost himself more and more in the depths of alcohol. My diary recorded the horrible night he tried breaking into the apartment with his knife.

Feb. 13: Danny returned home from going out with Paul last night so drunk that he staggered. He tried for 10 minutes to get into the house with a knife. Carved the door up pretty bad, then he went next door and nearly started on that one. I called him, and he came inside.

He sat in the chair about two hours until he wet all over himself. Then he started staggering around again and I guided him into his room. Finally he took off all his clothes and went to bed and I heard no more from him. He had a small bottle of liquor in his jacket which I poured out. I have finally made up my mind that he must go to a rehabilitation center.

Feb. 14: I called the lawyer today and he is going to try to find Danny a place to go. He didn't think the judge could approve a place out of state.

Feb. 19: Even though I talked to the lawyer twice last week, he didn't even find a place for Danny. Instead he's trying to get him a job at a place with Job Corp. Every time we go to see him, he asks to see Danny and I'm left sitting in the waiting room. I'm afraid we're going to have to straighten him out.

I'm getting so worn out with all this mess that I can scarcely cope with anything any longer. Jon suffers because of it. Danny has been extremely difficult to deal with. He's started verbally abusing me again and is disobedient. God, show us the right place for him. Don't let Satan have him, please.

I grew increasingly desperate as the deadline the judge had given us approached.

Feb. 21: I phoned the judge today and he doesn't have

any other place to recommend except programs costing as much as the hospital. He said I should see about Straight, and that he wasn't going to accept anything the lawyer had to offer.

Feb. 22: I contacted Straight and am supposed to be there Friday night at 6:15. The lady said they could take Danny March 1. This is his trial date. I have to see about Ken. Will he be willing to go? We have to attend Monday and Friday for three weeks, then once every other week for help for ourselves. It's going to cost a lot, but not as much as the hospital.

Ken exploded with rage when I told him about *another* drug program for our son. Money took priority with him. However I agreed to pay off the remainder of the hospital bill if he would sponsor Danny in the new drug program.

Then Ken raised the question that I had braced myself for when I came to ask him to help me with the finances for Straight. "I'll go with you to the place and if Danny enters it, help with the money, but I want you to come back home."

I looked at him for a long moment. Lines etched his drawn face and he'd lost weight. He looked like an unwanted stray dog. "OK," I said. "If the judge agrees to Danny going, I'll move back in with you." Inside I doubted that Danny would ever appreciate the sacrifice I had made for him that day.

Feb. 24: The lawyer called me yesterday and wants Danny to see a Job Corp employer. We have an appointment Monday morning. Ken has agreed to attend the Straight program orientation with me. I have worked nine hours a day the last four days trying to make up for the time I'll lose next week. God gives me strength for every day. Danny went out last night about 9:30 and didn't return until 1:00. I feared he was in jail again, but he had been drinking.

He is going to spend the night at David's, and Jon will stay with Grandma Cantrell when we go to Straight. The psychiatrist and the fellow from the Care Unit both called today, urging me to get help for Danny. God is leading.

I borrowed Mr. Wilks' station wagon to make the trip to Atlanta when Ken said he didn't think the Squareback could make the five-hour trip, and I didn't want to cause any needless antagonism between us. It felt strange to be alone with him. We talked very little as the miles sped by.

After getting "lost" for over an hour, we arrived as the sun set in a golden ball over what looked like a grocery store with the windows boarded-up. Cars streamed into the parking lot.

When my husband and I entered the front office, a friendly adult, who we later learned was a parent of one of the young people in the program, directed us to the "carpet room," a long room the length of the building with restrooms at one end. I noted three sets of double-doors leading into another room where I could hear young voices singing. A staff member helped us locate the group of guests waiting to view the program for the first time. She introduced us to our host couple.

The man and woman spoke kindly and reassuringly to us. A warmth like an overcoat on a winter's day enfolded me. Something about these people made me feel I had known them all my life. Nor did I feel like hiding behind my wall of pretense.

They hugged one another, and many were crying or talking intensely to one another. A food bar served sandwiches and juice to the parents.

A staff member caught everybody's attention and told us in what order we would go into the Open Meeting. Also that there would be no talking and everyone should keep their eyes on the speakers. Then he said, "Love you, Group," and they returned with, "Love you."

We filed into a room as large as a gymnasium to the strains of young people singing a wonderful song, "We Are Straight, We Are Invincible." Over the next months it would become a hauntingly beautiful embryo of life to me.

Ushered to folding chairs, we faced the young people: boys on one side and girls on the other. Hundreds of parents filed in. I studied the faces of the young people. They sat neatly dressed and groomed in jeans and shirts, their faces reminding me of a flower garden, ranging from bright sunflowers to drooping bleeding hearts.

The meeting, the people, the caring, left me breathless with excitement. No one until now had had any concern about how *I felt*. No one seemed to care that *I* hurt. I devoured the experience like a starved animal with a loaf of bread.

The meeting began with singing in which everybody took part. Several young people, new in the program, stood and gave their "introductions," telling what drugs they had done, setting goals for themselves, and relating what they were learning by being in the Straight program.

In my mind I visualized my son's face as each one spoke. My heart sang within me as tears flowed down my cheeks. To someday see Danny sitting in one of those chairs would fill my heart with unbounded joy.

Several young people graduated from the program. They were handsome, with a radiance and self-confidence that thrilled me. The parents stood with them, as parent and young person shared a little of what they had learned through the Straight program. *Would I ever see Danny standing like these young people, graduating as a straight person?*

Long before I wanted to leave, a young man ushered us out, along with our host couple, to a small room that served as our conference room. The host couple told us some of their story—how both they and their sons were going through an educational and healing process at Straight.

They explained that if Danny came, he would stay in the home of a parent whose child also belonged in the program. The couple would supply his room and board as if he were their own. The home might have up to ten young men "druggies."

The "foster" parent would bring him to the building each day for rap sessions to deal with feelings long repressed or only exhibited with anger. My son would have the opportunity to work his way through five steps of the program, each giving him more liberties, until he would return to school and work at a job.

Some young people had gone through the program in a matter of months, while for others it took several years.

Our host explained that we would support the family that Danny stayed with by a monthly check for room and board after he reached the first phase of his program. Until then we would not know the identity of his particular family, and he would have to earn the privilege of talking with us face to face. Instead he would speak to us only from the front of the group at the open meetings.

A staff member came and took down information about our son, then directed us to a hotel several miles away where the parents of young people enrolled in the program could get a room for a nominal price.

My watch said 12:15 when we reached the hotel. I felt like a bride as I slipped between the white sheets next to Ken. "What a fancy place," I commented.

"Yeah," he agreed, "we certainly couldn't have afforded this without the special rate!"

The heavy burden of so many months seemed to be lifting and it left me feeling light, young, and giddy.

After many months of negative entries, I entered a happy report of our trip into my diary.

Feb. 27: Ken and I went to Atlanta to Straight. It was so inspiring. There must have been 300 young people there. Now we will wait and see what the judge says. Straight is a wonderful place with wonderful caring people, and I know, "All things work together for good to those who love the Lord."

Feb. 28: Well, tomorrow is the day the Lord will show

us His will for Danny. I took him down to Job Corp today for his interview. It felt so hollow and uncaring compared to Straight. I took the Straight folder by to the judge. He was in his office and seemed grateful that I had brought it. Just in case I didn't see him, I had also written a note in which I told him some of what I had seen and heard at Straight and how it was where I wanted my son.

Danny is acting strange again, just like he did before his last trial. He is very quiet. I know he is wondering again what his future holds. It makes me sick to my stomach to think of going into the courtroom once more. I know he must feel even worse.

I left the materials about Straight on the kitchen table and told him to look them over. Matthew 6:34: "Take no thought for the morrow: for the morrow shall take thought for the things of itself."

I felt a strange calm as we came before the judge's bench. Ken and Danny seemed extremely subdued.

March 1: Today we went to court for, I hope, the last time ever. The judge asked the lawyer what he had decided for Danny. When the lawyer replied Job Corp or another job that was pending, the judge said sternly, "This boy needs more than a job. I suggest the four of you go into the hall and bring me a better solution if you don't want him in reform school."

The lawyer called Ken and me out and asked our opinion, and we concluded that Straight was to be the place. The judge said that Job Corp did not meet Danny's needs, that he needed an education, not a job.

The lawyer took Danny aside, and when they came back to the judge's bench, Danny said, "Judge Gray, I would like to go to Straight. I'd like to get my life together and quit stagnating." So, we will have a court order to that effect in a few days. God is wonderful. Praise His Name. He can do anything.

Danny had a lot of education ahead of him. He was not straight and seemed to want to keep his candle burning at both ends. My nerves were shot the next few days.

March 4: Mrs. Grubbs, a teacher at school, phoned last night and said Danny had given a boy a Pepsi with some kind of sleeping pill in it, and the principal had received a weird phone call they thought to be from Danny. She felt afraid he might be somewhere in bad shape. Scared me to death.

After searching for him more than an hour, I found him and his friend Paul parked near the Sonic Drive-in. Danny seemed full of something, beer I know. He angrily climbed into the car with me.

I have everything ready to move back home. God, I'm in Your hands, my family is in Your hands. We're trusting You to guide us, Father.

March 4: We returned home today. My dad and Danny hauled it all home in the press's van. Ken refused to help, commenting that he hadn't moved any of it over there in the first place. I couldn't have done it by myself. Danny did not seem to react to what was going on, though Jon seemed excited.

Boxes stood in disarray in every room. With no time to unpack, I threw clothes into suitcases for the trip to Atlanta. Following Straight's instructions, I marked all of Danny's things with his name. "I don't see why ya're doing all this," he repeated each time he entered his room. "Ya know I'm not goin' to be there that long!"

CHAPTER
8

ALL IN THE FAMILY

Come on, Mom, it's my last night. Why can't ya let me go see Paul? I'll be back early, I promise."

"No," I said for the hundredth time Friday evening. I didn't intend for him to get out of my sight, but as the evening wore on, his insistence wore me to the bone. Finally, exhausted from moving, preparing for the trip, and fearing all the time that Ken might change his mind, I finally told Danny to leave.

Eleven, 12:00, and 1:00 passed as I tossed in bed, too exhausted and fearful to sleep. My bedside clock read nearly 2:00 when the headlights of Paul's truck finally flashed across the bedroom wall. Still Danny didn't come into the house.

At 3:30 I slipped from the bed, wrapped myself warmly, and went outside. Danny's Chevy parked at the end of the driveway resembled a gray phantom in February's drizzling rain.

He sat like a robot in the front seat of the car. "Come to bed, Danny. It's only an hour until we leave." Opening the door, he all but fell into my arms. The aroma of marijuana, cigarettes, and alcohol made me nauseous.

Encouraging him to shower before he went to sleep, I returned to bed. I had scarcely shut my eyes when the alarm sounded.

Quickly scrambling eggs for sandwiches, I then fixed a thermos of orange juice and packed sandwiches for lunch along with snacks. We had borrowed Grandpa Cantrell's car. Ken and Jon loaded it with suitcases, a few toys for Jon, and the lunch.

Danny insisted on a shower when I finally managed to get him on his feet. When he didn't get to have his way, he stomped out of the house, lighting a cigarette on the way.

The trip to Atlanta took five hours. The first half sped quickly by as we slept fitfully. "Mom," Jon cried, "Danny knocked my glasses off."

When I reprimanded him, he grumbled, "That's right, take up for the little baby," throwing in foul language like confetti. Jon crouched in his corner, trying not to touch his brother.

"Dad, ya gotta stop. I need to go to the bathroom."

"Danny, I've stopped twice already, we're suppose ta be there by 9:00. How ya think we're gonna make it if we have ta stop every half hour for you? We stop for you more than Jon."

A volley of cursing followed, Ken adding his share, but ultimately we halted every half-an-hour to forty-five minutes. Each time I smelled alcohol as Danny settled into his seat again.

We made our last rest stop at a gas station as we turned off the interstate. Even though I had brought along plenty to drink and eat, Danny asked me for money.

"No, we're nearly there. You don't need anything. Get in, there's plenty to eat in here."

"Did ya ever think I just might want somethin' else?" His face flushed red and felt too close to mine.

The name calling along with the cursing began once more, Ken getting into it also. "Will both of you quiet down? Don't you see people watching us? Get in, Danny. You too, Ken."

Danny slammed his door, producing another outburst

from his father, who jerked the car into gear. I scarcely noted Jon's small form in his little corner of the back seat.

We walked into the front office of the Straight organization like a row of wooden soldiers, hostilities smoldering like red coals covered by ashes. It looked like any office with a desk and some chairs. We gave our name and reason for coming. A young girl about Danny's age (referred to as a runner, I later learned), took a note beyond the closed doors. In a few minutes a staff member and two young men beckoned us inside.

The young men invited Danny to go with them down one hall while Ken, Jon, and I went with the staff member to another (intake) room that was set up with a table and chairs for our orientation into the Straight program. He explained to us that the young men would talk with Danny, encouraging him to sign into the program of getting himself drug free.

Three other couples who had brought young people sat around the table. The morning sped by as we filled out forms and listened to an orientation lecture from a staff member who also had a young person in the program.

"Sorry, Danny's evidently been drinking. We want to wait until he's more sober before asking him to sign himself in." The director bent over where Ken and I were busily completing forms. "The boys have taken the liquor he had in his pocket, although he'd already consumed most of it. He won't need these cigarettes either, if you'd like to dispose of them."

Several times in the early afternoon she returned to give us the same report. Finally at 4:00, after all the other parents had left, she told us that our son had signed himself in.

We walked out of our intake room into another where we met him. The same two guys were with him. Danny came and hugged me real hard, tears flowing down his face and mine. Ken held out his hand and they shook weakly.

"Dad, you're going to have to work on those affections." The director gave my husband a gentle hug.

We had called ahead for reservations at the same hotel where Ken and I stayed the first time we came to view the program. The staff members encouraged us to go there, relax, and return on Monday evening for the Open Meeting.

Relax! How could I relax? Months and years of tension had left me as taut as a fishing line with a hundred-pound bass at the other end, and more nervous than boiling water. But sleep actually came like gentle rain on parched ground. I couldn't get enough. For the first time in months I didn't have to lie awake listening for an unsteady knock on the door or the phone with a police officer at the other end. Nor did I have to wonder if Danny had killed someone or was even dead himself.

The park adjoining the hotel, filled with azaleas and dogwoods, made an ideal place for walking. Jon, Ken, and I breathed in the crisp spring air.

The weekend went by in a blur of eating and sleeping. I reveled in it like a child in a swimming pool on a hot summer's day. *Can this be true? Am I really living this? Don't I have to be doing something about Danny right now?* I kept asking myself.

Monday evening we made our way to the "building" — as we would call it in future months. We left Jon in the front office under the watchful eye of the secretary who was one of the parents in the program, having mistakenly brought him along, not knowing that parents were the only ones to attend Open Meetings for the first two weeks.

Parents and guests milled quietly in the "carpet" room. A staff member directed us to the "new parent" group where we found familiar faces. The three couples who had been through intake with us Saturday morning waved a cheery hello. We laughed together as we shared the fact that we all looked less haggard than we had then.

As we filed into the Open Meeting, I searched the boys' side of the ones in the program. Danny sat on the front row, staring straight ahead. His long shaggy hair now shown clean and shiny in a shorter style. He wore it parted on the side. His neatly buttoned Ivy League yellow shirt and clean jeans made him look like he'd just stepped out of a catalog.

A picture of him before he began doing drugs flashed through my mind. Suddenly I wanted to run to him and enfold him in my arms. I longed to stand on the chair and shout, "Look, my son is here. Doesn't he look great?" Ken stared at his son in disbelief.

We soon learned that we were a vital part of his recovery. For the first month of the program we attended two meetings a week and then as appointed by the staff.

"Don't expect your child to be one bit stronger than you yourself are," the staff member emphasized over and over. He explained that if we entered wholeheartedly into the program and gained from it the necessary insights, we in turn could be a better support to our son.

"You can't keep your child straight. He will have to make that choice daily. There are no miracle cures. Each day, after your son or daughter graduates, it will be his or her choice alone if he or she does drugs."

Open Meeting amazed me. For an average of three hours we sat listening to joyful or furious, fearful or turned-on children and adults. During this time no one left the room, talked unless from the microphone or up front, ate, drank, or took their eyes off the person speaking.

Through it all I gained insight into my own life by listening to others. I learned new respect for the art of speaking that carried over into my church and work activities. It felt good to look a person straight in the eyes when communicating and gave me a new sense of confidence.

During Open Meeting I found it difficult to keep my eyes off my son, but the staff had instructed us not to play eye games. To catch a son or daughter's eye and see the self-pity brooding could prompt a parent to pull the "poor little child" from the program.

The Straight program also requested its participants, including parents and siblings, to dress conservatively, avoiding such things as shorts and low-cut dresses.

Each family must always be within phone contact. We could not plan vacations until the child had progressed to a higher phase, and then only with special permission.

At the Open Meeting we stood as the parent next to us passed the microphone. Then we would tell how we felt about Danny and his actions either in the past or the present.

Each parent said something to their child. Some of the comments were encouraging while others were at times disheartening. Danny gave his "introduction" for the following four weeks, each time relating something about his past and his goals for the future.

When Ken and I had to speak, my voice cracked with emotion. "I feel good about you being here, Danny. I hope you'll soon be home. I love you."

"I'm angry, but I love you, Danny," my husband said.

Tears ran down our son's cheeks as he faced us. "Love you, Mom. Love you, Dad," he managed to get out, then sat down as we did. The young people in the program chorused, "Love you, Danny."

After the Open Meeting, the adults walked to different intake or conference rooms for raps, many of them conducted by parents in higher phases of the program. Siblings attended their own sessions.

Later when Jon began going to the Open Meeting, I felt apprehensive about him attending his own rap session. An older parent in the program quickly explained that the siblings watched out for one another.

In the intake room, our instructor assured us our children were also doing a rap on the evening's meeting. We shared our feelings about each of our children's introductions.

Although I told Danny that first evening I hoped he could come home soon, I didn't honestly want him back. I didn't want to resume the "hell" of a drug addict in my home again. Instead I longed for a straight son who could laugh and play, one with ambition enough to finish his education and hold a job. Most of all I wanted a son whom I could love and respect, one who could feel the same for me.

Our first rap session began a new concept for each of us, including Jon. We began writing a "Moral Inventory" each day for the duration of the program. A diary had been a part of my life for several years, but this one gave me a new-found freedom.

We took a problem from our day, then decided why it was a problem, how it affected ourselves and others, what happened in our lives if we changed or didn't change it, and how it helped us personally. Next we were to work out, individually, on paper, how we intended to change it.

The Moral Inventory became a daily part of my life, as well as that of each of the other families. Each day I wrote in my notebook a specific problem. Some days brought more problems than others, and I wrote more than one MI. I used steps similar to that of Alcoholics Anonymous. First I had to admit my powerlessness over the problem and believe that a Power greater than myself could restore me to sanity. I had to turn my will and life over to God's care as I understood Him. The next step brought a searching and fearless moral inventory of myself as I admitted to God, myself, and another human being the exact nature of my wrongs. I made direct amends wherever possible except when to do so might injure them, myself, or others. Through prayer and meditation I sought to improve my conscious contact with God, praying only for knowledge of His will for me and the Power to carry that out. Once I had received the gift of awareness, I practiced these principles in all my daily affairs and carried the message to all that I felt I could help.

Three signs prominently displayed around the headquarters building brought order and discipline into my life as I practiced what they urged: "Think, think, think," "First things first," and "Easy does it."

The Serenity Prayer gave me strength and comfort a hundred times a day as I repeated, "God grant me the serenity to accept the things I cannot change, the courage to change the things I can, and the wisdom to know the difference."

The Straight program stressed five guidelines to base every decision on. I must decide everything grounded on objective reality, the protection of my own life, the need to produce goals, the desire to feel and act the way that I need to, and the avoidance of trouble with others.

The program became a wonderful way of living. I reveled in the new freedom I felt. *I am a person,* I thought, *I can be me!* I learned to use love and forgiveness where once I knew only anger and frustration. Gradually I discovered how to place my life and my relationships in their proper order to maintain a new level of love, understanding, compassion, and honesty.

Fortunately I didn't have to carry the burden alone. My trust in God had always been strong, but now I realized that I was trying to handle my burdens instead of letting Him have charge of them. In the words of a phrase that I often repeated, I learned to let go and let God.

The first of many MIs I would write declared:

Mar. 8: Challenge: I will stop trying to manipulate other people's lives. I have been doing this because I feel frightened that things won't go right otherwise. It makes me frustrated and antagonizes others. If I keep it up I will drive away those close to me. Now I can relax and watch them grow. And I can relax too, remembering that only God can work change in a person's life. Instead I will be content with things (persons) as they are.

Good Points: I am unselfish. I like others to be happy even if it means sacrificing my own happiness. A caring person, I dislike seeing people unhappy if I can remedy it.

Good Things: I scratched my husband's back. When I didn't get to eat out, I didn't become angry about it.

Goals: I'll try to share my feelings more with my husband. I will let others work out their own problems, helping only if asked.

Blessings: I'm thankful for God's mercy in leading us to Straight. I'm thankful for being part of raps. I'm thankful I have my family together again.

Ken's first MI read: *Challenge:—When I feel unconcerned about what others think of what I do or say, I hurt myself and others. This attitude alienates people from me. A better attitude will bring the same people back, not alienate me from them. I admit that I am powerless over this challenge.*

Good Points: I try to be a perfectionist. I'm a good worker.

Goals: I will talk to my family about my challenge.

Blessings: I'm thankful for my family. I'm thankful for my life. I'm thankful for my health.

Jon, with my help, printed his first MI several weeks later:

I challenge myself to think before I speak. I do this because I don't stop to think. I am powerless over this problem. I am turning it over to God. I hurt others' feelings and am disrespectful which makes me feel sad. Dear Lord, help me to think before I speak. I will think, think, think before I speak.

Good Points: I did my math well. I am patient. I like animals.

Goal: To think before I speak. And I will share.

Dear Jesus, I'm thankful for the snow, and I'm thank-

ful for my teacher. I'm thankful for my friends at school. I'm thankful for my mom and dad and Fluffy, my cat. I'm thankful for my dog Spice. I'm thankful for my brothers. I'm thankful for Jesus and God. I love you, Jon.

And Danny, also, wrote a daily MI with the assistance of a young man who had been in the program longer. His first one read:

Challenge: I challenge myself to be more specific. I need to be more specific because I am too general in my relations to the group. I am also insecure about digging down into myself for the different specific things I need to talk about. I am going to make a change in this area by taking my time in my thoughts and digging into my feelings and bringing out specific things I need to talk about.

Goals: I will talk about the time I went camping when my mom told me, No. I will learn my 6th step tonight because I will get called on in group tomorrow.

Good Points: I have love for others. I am sympathetic. I am sensitive.

Blessings: I am thankful for seeing my mother tonight and being able to tell her truthfully that I love her.

Good Points: Love. Tonight I truly felt love toward my mother and the rest of the parents because they love us so much. I can't help returning this love with more love. Sympathy. I felt sympathy today when I heard others going through their feelings about the things they have done in their past. I have had some of the same things happen to me. Sensitivity. I felt a lot of sensitivity today toward others in my group when they expressed their feelings. I felt as though I was going through the same feelings with them.

Two weeks later Jon went with us into the Open Meeting for the first time. As we stood to face Danny, our youngest son rose with us. His brother's eyes flooded with tears as Jon said, "You're looking good. I love you, Danny."

Constantly borrowing cars to make the trip to Atlanta became more than we wanted to do, so Ken decided to trade in the Squareback for a Nissan. Shopping around, we found a yellow car that Ken and I both liked.

We laughed together as we made the trip home in the new car. I learned the gears, popped the trunk open instead of the hood, and tried out all the gadgets like a teenager. A fragile bridge of communication showed signs of forming between Ken and me. It was fun to shop and enjoy laughing with him.

Nervously I awaited the next trip to Straight in three weeks, hoping Danny would advance to the "Talk" stage. It would mean that we could speak with him after the Open Meeting and several times during the weekend.

April 4: I received the best phone call today that I have had in years about Danny. His counselor called and gave me a list of his "stash" he wanted to get rid of: his car, jacket, tapes, and rock records, also some pot roaches and seeds he had hidden in his car. It makes me so happy knowing it's coming from him. I thank God. Hebrews 10:23: "He is faithful that promised." Praise His name!

April 11: I felt so disappointed Danny didn't get Talk. I had just known he would. When we spoke to him over the mike, I told him I felt disappointed. Then Ken agreed with what I said and added that he was behind him 100%. He said again that he hoped Danny understood that he supported him 100%. Lights went on in Danny's eyes and he cried. I cried through the rest of the meeting. I know Danny needed to hear what Ken said more than anything!

EASY DOES IT

After nearly two months I finally touched my new son. The old feelings of love and care were still all there. My heart leaped with joy. Later I recorded the happy moments in my diary.

Apr. 29: Danny got Talk privileges. He looked pale as he ran toward us, hugging Ken first and then me, and finally Jon. His crying told us that he had clearly missed us.

After Open Meeting, we met for 15 minutes with him. Again he cried a lot as he told me of being sorry for his actions at the apartment and for knocking Jon out of the bed the night he came in drunk. He apologized to Ken for giving him bad times, and Ken cried along with Danny. They hugged each other again. Jon sat frightened and sad. Afterward he said he had a big lump in his throat.

"This evening I want you to show me exactly where your son or daughter was in their drug use before coming to Straight." The staff mother passed out sheets of paper to us for our rap session after Open Meeting. "Do you know a child can become an alcoholic in two to three years? It can take an adult up to 20 years.

"People feel normal most of the time. Our lives are normal with work, recreation, sleep, etc. Now and then we suffer pain when we have a death, a divorce, or a disinterested parent. Euphoria occurs less often: falling in love, getting to drive a car for the first time, or the first date."

As the evening proceeded, I learned Danny's first stage of chemical dependency began in experimental use. The chart the woman had passed out showed pain on one side, euphoria on the other, and normal in the center.

In the experimental stage Danny had discovered how to swing from normal into euphoria by employing a chemical. During this time period I hadn't known he was using anything except the incident of his taking the first pill.

Like riding a bicycle for the first time, chemicals were challenging and exciting. Taking them eased the pain of his problems with his father at home, and his insecure feelings at school, with few consequences.

As he entered the second stage, he began riding the bicycle of drugs like an expert two-wheeler. He learned that chemicals produced good feelings that he liked and sought after. At this point he still controlled the drugs. He began at normal on the scale, went into euphoria, but still came down low on the normal scale.

"Danny, why don't you take a shower this morning?"

"Aw, Mom, quit bugging me. I'm fine."

"Well, how about wearing a clean shirt? That one looks as if you got it from the dirty clothes hamper!"

"Just stop it. I told ya I'm OK!"

But now his dress and appetite were changing, he began verbal abuse toward me, and his respect for God dropped drastically. *What's going on with Danny?* I had wondered. *It must be just another phase of puberty.* As a result I cautioned, disciplined, and got extremely angry with his lying, skipping school, and bad choices of friends.

Actually my son didn't know how much alcohol and pot were enough. One marijuana cigarette was too many and a thousand not enough. He experienced losses for the first time. His straight friends no longer accepted him, his relationship with his family deteriorated, and his integrity wilted under the blast of drugs.

As Danny entered the third stage of drug use, his mood swing began as normal, barely going into euphoria, and ending in pain after he'd dropped a couple of hits of speed. By now he had to employ drugs just to feel good and avoid feeling bad from new feelings caused by truancy, depression, and loss of control.

"Danny, where is your camera? I haven't seen you using it lately."

"Oh, I let Jeff borrow it. Guess he's forgot to return it."

In actuality, he had hocked the camera to get money for drugs, but he couldn't remember for sure what he'd done with it. Soon he couldn't remember what he'd done for hours at a time because of black-outs in which his memory turned off while his body remained functioning.

Getting phone calls from the police, I took responsibility for most of the consequences, with Danny fighting me and the law. His conflicts with his dad became violent.

"You'll stop playing that rock music so loud when ya come up the drive. I could hear it a mile away." Ken shook his finger in his son's face.

"It's my car, and I can do as I please." Danny turned and defiantly retreated, slamming the back door.

His father followed him into the yard. "Did ya hear what I said? I expect you to obey!"

"Ah, go to _____ ."

Ken picked up a lawn chair and slung it at him with all his might. Danny caught the other end with his hand. The two men began a tug-of-war. Five minutes later the chair lay in shambles, dust hung in the air from Danny's exit in the Chevy, and Ken stalked toward the barn to avoid me.

During stage four Danny's mood swing no longer brought him euphoria. Instead it began in pain, barely went into normal, and returned to pain. Now he experienced frequent trouble with the police and school and had no job. Several times he had run away, but his disease packed its bag and followed him. His self-esteem had vanished, leaving him paranoid and filled with bad feelings about himself.

"Now where do you picture your child?" the Straight instructor continued. My mind had been racing through the past three years. Glancing at the paper, I realized the nightmare he had lived during phase four.

Apr. 30: We talked to Danny again this afternoon. His paleness was gone and he looked so happy as he came toward us. He hugged us all. His first words were, "I felt happy with our talk Friday night."

He talked of the vacation to the Smokies and how he had stolen $60.00 from his father, had an old man buy him some liquor, and then drank it alone in the motel. Now he said that he had felt so lonely, and expressed sorrow for the hurt he had caused us. He told Ken he was sorry about stealing his money, and Jon that he was disappointed for not being the right example as a brother and wanted another chance. Jon got up and hugged him. As Danny rose to go, he told his father that he felt proud of the changes he saw in him. Danny looks good and has gained some weight. He wore the new jeans we had taken for him Fri. night.

May 13: We went to Atlanta and Danny got "Coming Home." It felt like birthdays and Christmases rolled into one. When we stood to speak, Danny hollered, "Coming Home." He hugged us all at once.

Although we had talked with Danny 15 minutes at a time, we had not been alone together. "Coming Home" meant he could now spend any extra time he had away from his raps as well as his nights with us when we were in Atlanta.

After hugging us, Danny returned to his chair with the other guys in the program. Open Meeting continued.

Early morning finally found us finished with our raps and Danny with his. Meeting in the front office, we hugged one another. "I feel scared," he commented. The Straight program had already taught him to admit his feelings up front.

As Ken drove us to the hotel, we chattered like a bunch of monkeys. Danny couldn't stop talking. His face wore a soft, tender expression, and he reached out often to touch my shoulder, to pat Ken's arm, and to hug Jon.

The process of unburdening the guilt that had caused so much of his anger in his past, continued at the hotel. He confessed stealing a large amount of money after breaking into his grandparents' home while we were all sitting in church.

Going over the events of the previous Christmas brought tears of remorse running down his ruddy cheeks. "All those wasted years," he repeated over and over in bitter disappointment.

At 9:00 the next morning we hugged Danny goodbye as Ken sped him toward the Straight program headquarters for his rap sessions.

Now that we knew where Danny lived, I phoned his foster parents' home, and because of the woman's insistence, we went to their home to spend another night. This evening began the first of many such experiences.

Her husband had the boys home by 10:00. Saturday nights were a special togetherness time, I learned. Danny had with him a new boy in the program. I sensed he felt very proud of this fact.

The boys ate with gusto the meal their foster mother had fixed for them and afterward began writing their MIs. They shared feelings that they had experienced with one another, took showers, then we made fruited milk shakes for each of them.

Later, in the living room, we all sat in a circle and played charades. I turned over and over trying to depict bacon. Ken's catfish imitation was hilarious as he meowed and swam simultaneously.

Our evening ended past midnight as the host father asked our son to read from the Bible. He read the 23rd psalm and remarked that it had been the first book he had opened in two months. His prayer consisted of simple and beautiful words of thanks and trust.

Danny slept on a makeshift bed in our room. Although he could have shared the large attic room with the rest of the boys, he wanted to be with us. We sat on the bed as he rid himself of more guilt that he had bottled up within him for so long.

Sunday morning brought more sharing as we ate a lovely breakfast at the large dining table. I drank it all in like a hungry kitten with a dish of warm milk.

The host parents discussed everything in a loving and honest way. Some of the things the boys expressed from their pasts brought tears to my eyes. They sought to define their angry feelings as hurt, disappointment, or a hundred other honest emotions. Such sharing brought them intense relief. I wanted the same experience for my own home.

The rest of the morning Ken, Danny, Jon, and I spent downstairs where the parents had a pool table, various exercise machines, and a pinball machine. Ken and I played with the boys like we were children again.

May 15: We departed for home as the guys left for the building at 1:15. If I could have taken one five-minute period from this whole wonderful weekend, I'd have chosen when Danny read from the Bible and prayed. It is the greatest weekend I've had.

May 30: We just got one night this time. Danny seemed much more relaxed. He felt discouraged about not making phase 3, but he did admit he hadn't been consistent in raps.

As our son worked on the phases of his program, so did we on ours. During each of our rap sessions at the Straight program we learned more and more about ourselves.

June's summer colors were vivid hues of green when we visited Danny at a new foster home. Finding him watching TV instead of wanting to talk, I felt distant from him. The new foster parents didn't seem as strict as those in the former home.

Finally he reached phase three and was now eligible to begin school. I brought his transcript with me so his foster parents could enroll him in a high school nearby.

Five days later the staff put him back to phase two. Also they took him out of school and put him in another home. Somehow I wasn't surprised and knew that the staff had made a good decision.

June 27: Danny hollered, "Coming back home, 3rd phase," in Open Meeting. He acted so much better, more in touch with himself.

Danny became more perceptive of our feelings with each trip that we made to see him. One evening, early in July, several young men of 20 or 21 did their introductions. They reminded me so much of David that I longed for him to see his brother and the good things that were happening to him, and I cried each time I noticed them.

As soon as we reached the car, Danny asked, "What's wrong, Mom?" After I told him, he put his arms around me and also cried. He talked about how much he cared for his brother David.

June 27: Later, before we went to bed, Danny talked to Ken and asked him to define his angry feelings and see what they were: hurt, frustration, disappointment, or what? He said that when Ken withholds his feelings from David, it is like taking David's very soul. His father must relate to him and save him.

For several weeks I begged David to visit the Straight program with us, explaining that his sister Anita and her husband, Randy, planned to meet us for a weekend in July. Although he always replied, "No thanks," I continued to pressure him until he said "Maybe."

July 22: Forty-five minutes before we were to leave for Straight, David called and said he'd go with us. Ken didn't want him going, but when we picked David up, no tension filled the car like it would have in the past.

Anita and Randy met us at the hotel. We got two rooms

because David can't be with Danny because of his own drug use. Because Danny was still at the building, the rest of us went for a swim and had supper. At the Straight building, the staff had time to interview only Anita, so Randy and David didn't get to go in to view the program.

Anita seemed fascinated with the Open Meeting. Her mouth fell open when she spotted Danny in the group. Because David was doing drugs, the staff did not allow him to talk to his brother. It made me feel sad, but I knew it was in Danny's best interest, since David had shared drugs with his brother several times, even the night Ken and I had come for our first interview at Straight.

The weekend mingled both sadness and happiness for me. Happiness as I saw Danny's progress and his reunion with his sister and brother-in-law, sadness as I felt David's alienation and frustration at his exclusion from, and lack of understanding of, the program at Straight. Not loving David any less for "using," I only felt pain for him.

Later the following day several of the staff interviewed Randy and David. They approved Randy's participation, but not David. The staff encouraged him to go to Alcoholics Anonymous for a month and then return for another interview. If it didn't check out drug free, he should put himself into the program.

While Danny spent time at the building on Saturday, the rest of the family visited with Lois, my girlfriend who had moved to Atlanta. I felt special as I shared with her all the wonderful things happening with Danny.

David seemed reserved throughout the afternoon, his mind off somewhere else, although Lois's boys, whom David had grown up with, were chattering away at him.

When we arrived back at the hotel, he vomited several times, something I'd never seen him do unless he had a virus. That evening Anita said she had observed him crying. Although I stayed with Danny and the family, I longed to be with the tall, handsome young man in the other room.

The following day, after our Goodbyes, we began our trip home in the rain. When the wipers on the car quit, David and Ken worked on them together. Never before had I seen my husband work side by side with David, talking to his son as if he were an equal. The scene exhilarated me.

David never went to AA. Instead he chose to continue working with his Uncle Leo and making a life for himself. His forgiving spirit and self-determination eventually led him to marriage, a comfortable home, and the security and love that were the two things he wanted most.

Danny's junior year at a high school near his foster parents brought good grades as he applied himself to everything offered. A parent in the program drove him to school and to his new job.

One summer afternoon we visited him at the fast-food restaurant where he worked. He looked so bright and handsome as he dumped a batch of fries into the loading bin.

Aug. 14: Danny liked the watch we gave him for his birthday.

After we had driven the car to the front of the Hilton Hotel, Ken, Jon, and I began unloading the suitcases. My husband reached for the cake-carrier containing the spice cake decorated with yellow icing. As he handed it to me, the cake-carrier fell apart, sending the spice cake sprawling in the center of the walkway leading into the hotel. For a moment I stood transfixed in horror, then began laughing.

A fancy hotel with an upside-down spice cake decorating its center walkway. Passersby looked on in disbelief as I scooped the cake into my hands and righted it on the cake-carrier while Jon ran for paper toweling to clean the yellow icing from the sidewalk.

Later, in our room, I scraped icing off the top, brought icing up from the sides to cover the bare spot, and reset the layers. Then the three of us laughed again. What a special birthday cake!

Aug. 16: Danny made fourth phase. He gets three days off a week, can write and receive mail, and can make phone calls. He called us himself.

STRAIGHT THINKING

Mom, do you think you're an enabler?" The question from the Straight instructor caught me off guard. (The instructor, whom we referred to as "Dad," called each of us mothers present, "Mom.")

"Well, I have no idea."

"Tonight," he continued, "we will discover the part each of you plays in the life of a chemically dependent person.

"By the way, do you know that you can be a dry-alcoholic? You can have all the attitudes of chemically-dependent behavior, such as denial of feelings, dishonesty, and the lack of willingness to communicate. Attitudes make up one-half of the chemically dependent person's problem, mind-altering drugs being the other half."

As Ken's head bowed in thought, I knew we were both thinking the same thing. The description fit him like a glove. Although he didn't do any drugs except tobacco, he was a druggie—a dry-druggie.

"You see," the instructor explained, "each of us has within us anger, pain, hurt, guilt, shame, and fear. The way in which we exhibit, or fail to exhibit, these feelings identifies us in the family circle."

During the evening I learned that each of our family

members fit a specific spot. The **chemically dependent** person in our family directed his attention outward so he wouldn't have to focus on himself. He did this by erecting a wall of defense composed of anger to cover up his number-one feeling of pain. Drug use is clearly a disease of the feelings.

I had seen Danny, the druggie child, exhibit compulsive behavior in conning me, and in being aggressive. At the time he entered the program he felt trapped in his self-delusion and no longer knew what a true feeling was.

"Danny, I'm missing several checks from my checkbook."

"So, what's it ta me?"

"Have you used them?"

"Mom, ya know I don't go nosin' around with your stuff."

He had forged my name on them and written them for cash at a local store, yet lied to me face to face. His integrity sank into the quicksand of drugs.

I found myself to be the classic **enabler**, providing the responsibility Danny liked in his life. For example, I called for him to give excuses when he didn't go to work, or when he skipped school. Yet at the same time I covered up my seething anger for having to be both mom and dad, and for the self-blame and self-pity I felt powerless to overcome. As a result I became super responsible for my druggie son.

"Hello. No, he isn't here right now. May I take a message?"

"This is the plant calling. Danny hasn't reported to work for two days, and we thought he might be ill."

"Well, he has had a cold. I will tell him to call you the minute he comes in."

Actually I hadn't seen my son for three days and had no idea as to his physical condition. But I lied, covered up, and enabled him to continue being a druggie. Instead of confronting him, I just thanked the Lord each time he came home.

Ken, the **passive adult** or **lost child**, withdrew to hide his never-ending rage. He felt more comfortable being distant and aloof. Although he considered himself to be super independent, yet he also felt rejected by me and other members of the family. My husband existed half-way in and half-way out of the family.

"Ken, it's your folks. Why can't they eat over here on Christmas Eve?"

"They can find someplace else to eat. I'm not running a restaurant."

Many times I planned events without his consent. The results were usually catastrophic with him slamming doors, turning out lights, cursing under his breath, and making everyone feel extremely uncomfortable.

Anita took the role of **hero** by providing the self-worth of the family through attending college and seeming to have it all-together, but at the same time desperately needing approval. Within, Anita felt guilty for the actions of her family. If she could look good enough, the family would appear better. In a sense she assumed the role of parent. While coming across as if she had it all-together, she never talked with others about the problems at home and seldom asked friends home with her because of the shame of it all.

Many times she took my burdens, trying to fix Ken and me, trying to fix David and Ken, and trying to fix Danny and the family. She let herself be stretched as far as she could go in all directions.

"You guys need to help Mom more. Can't you see the garbage needs taking out, your room is a mess, and the dishes still haven't been done?"

Anita potty-trained Jon, she often censored David and Danny, and she lashed out at her father when he spoke or treated me unkindly. Her five-foot-three-inch stance of authority stood tall among her brothers.

David assumed the **scapegoat** role by providing a focus away from Danny. Within him dwelt a great hurt that he covered with drugs and a defiant attitude. He withdrew from the family, feeling that what he did, not what he was, made the difference in his acceptance. His sense of belonging had been destroyed.

Afraid of his father, he took the blame for much of the disfunction of our family. More vocal, he expressed his growing anger at authority. Yet his strong peer values drove him to crave a family of his own. David ran like a scapegoat with Ken and me pointing our fingers at him.

"Mom, can't I drive?" Sixteen-year-old David longed to get behind the wheel of the VW. His father had allowed him to drive the tractor on occasion.

"OK, you can begin tomorrow," I said.

"No, he won't. He's not driving my car." Ken slammed his fist on the table.

David did drive, but not when his father knew about it. After we turned the corner beyond the driveway, I scooted over and allowed him the wheel. Such an exciting experience for a young man became tarnished by knowing that his father had said No and having his mother defy his dad's authority. To deal with it, he accepted himself as the blame for his mother having to lie for him and for his father not trusting him.

Jon slipped into the role of **mascot** and provided a distraction for the rest of the family. He disguised his fear through clowning and being hyperactive, anything to get our attention away from the problem with Danny. Sometimes he'd be so funny we'd laugh, at other times we'd want to punish him. One could describe him as a stick person holding out his hands between Ken and me.

"Mrs. Cantrell, I sent Jon to the principal's office today. He stabbed another little boy in the arm with a pencil. The principal has had a strong talk with him, and I'm sure you will follow through."

"Jon, what caused you to want to do this?"

"Mommy, I didn't mean to hurt him. He dared me to."

"You must not play around like this. It will cause you a lot of trouble as you go through school."

"I know, Mommy, I only wanted to have fun with

him." He crawled up in my lap and laid his head on my shoulder. "I didn't mean to hurt him, Mom."

As I listened to the Straight counselors, I wondered how anyone could know so much about my family. I felt like an X-ray probed deep within each of our hearts and exposed their secrets.

Now I understood why Anita protected me. She tried to be the mother that I should have been. I knew why David ran so many times, never being sure of his own identity in the family. And Jon with his monkey behavior asking for acknowledgment that he belonged in the family too.

Although we didn't put the pot or alcohol into our son's mouth, the attitudes of my family contributed toward his need for codependent support outside of our family group.

Suddenly I felt wonderfully free, like a dove flying from an imprisoning cage. *I had feelings, my children had feelings, and even Ken had feelings, buried under our exterior attitudes.* Feelings—the word had a smooth and exciting ring to it, like tasting an exotic dessert for the first time. *Now I could express myself and not worry about others getting defensive.* It was an exciting thought.

That evening I said, "I feel concerned," so many times that Danny finally asked, "Mom, don't you know any other feeling words?" We both laughed. It felt good to say how I felt, and I made the most of it. I liked the clean-inside-out feeling it gave me, like hanging a white wash on the clothesline on a summer day.

Bright orange and brown leaves crunched under my feet as I walked up into the hills alone one autumn day. For the first time in 20 years, I felt a burning need to get to know "me." I had avoided myself for so long that I had forgotten that I existed. Strangely enough, I had controlled everyone's life except my own.

Crossing the creek on the tree log, I passed the spring with its watercress growing in shiny green bunches. Winding my way through the maples, oaks, and elms, I found myself at the top of the large hill overlooking our valley. There I sat on a tree stump as I chewed on a sassafras twig. Our collie, Spice, lay at my feet, contentedly surveying the expanse.

"Who am I and what do I want out of life?" The question struck my mind like a returning boomerang.

While I had an excellent job, I never asserted myself. I never gave my opinion as to what kind of article might make a good one for our publication, or what type of contest might create more reader interest. Instead I just did my job as asked, allowing Mr. Wilks to dictate the contents of the magazine.

I'll apply myself more as an editor, I decided. *I'll learn more English, take some classes to better myself.* Now I felt excited. *And how about doing something good for yourself personally? Supper can wait. I'll begin a new walking program, exercise each morning. I may even go shopping once a week to give myself some relaxation!*

Who am I? The thought kept me busy for several weeks. Excitedly, I became reacquainted with me. *I can do anything, I am strong.* Yes, I was growing from an embryo to a newborn—discovering self.

"Mr. Brewer, I'm glad you could meet with me, and you, too, Truman. I've brought some popcorn the Booster Club for Straight is selling. Please buy as many as you like. I'm here to talk with you about the program at Straight."

I began to give talks at various schools and took brochures and told them to pass them on to needy parents like myself. My mission was to encourage parents not to get trapped into helping a codependent child. To encourage them to seek available help at the first onset of a problem with their young person. Everywhere I shared my story of Danny and of my helplessness and frustration.

"Mrs. Cantrell, I hope you can help me." Patty sat with downcast eyes. She had asked to speak with me shortly after I arrived at my office. "The kids I'm running with are doing drugs. What can I do? I haven't done any yet, but I feel scared."

"Patty, if you want to stay straight, you'll have to choose new friends. Don't be afraid of hurting the feelings of those you're running with. They'll find someone else and not even miss you. I'm proud of you for caring for yourself enough not to do drugs. Take care of yourself."

"Elaine, how can I help my brother-in-law? He's drinking more and more."

"He'll have to see his own need for help. This article will help you to understand what part the family needs to play. Why don't you and your family think about going to Al-Anon? It will teach each of you how to deal with yourself and the alcoholic."

Each week people came asking for help with their problems. While I didn't have the answers, I did have a positive attitude that attracted them. My growing ability to take good care of myself and my own life made others as curious as a cat hunting a mouse.

Now I felt like a butterfly who had finally emerged out of his cocoon on a beautiful summer's day. Able to make plans and carry them out, dream dreams and fulfill them, I felt happy and fulfilled. Many problems remained unsolved, but one problem dissipated slowly—me.

While I knew I couldn't stop Ken's tempermental outbursts, couldn't change his dry-alcoholic attitudes, I could do something just as important—take care of *me*.

PEACEFUL VALLEY

It's good to see you again, Nana. Hi, Papa." Danny bounded up the redwood porch giving bear hugs to his grandparents.

"Oh, Danny, you look so good." Tears of joy glistened in all of our eyes.

"Oh, Grandma and Grandpa, I'm so happy to be home." He stood like a quarterback, hugging both grandparents.

Grandpa removed his cap and scratched his bald head the way he always did when making plans. "Boy, you can do anything now. You can get on to college since you got rid of your bad habits."

Pages of happy memories began filling the spiral notebook. Danny's first trip home from the Straight program was special.

Oct. 27: After Open Meeting we left for home with Danny and a straight buddy of his in a higher phase of the program. Danny kept saying, "I feel so excited." We slept most of the way, with Ken driving. Got home about 3:00 a.m. Slept a few hours."

"We'll be late to church. Get up guys."

"No problem," Danny responded, his feet hitting the floor.

A youth choir sang the "Invocation" as we entered. I

felt like I wore the bronze medal from the Olympics. Young people in the choir began recognizing Danny. Bending like saplings in a windstorm, they whispered to each other of his presence.

Danny reveled in his hour. His smile and laughing eyes told me that he knew they were talking about him.

Oct. 28: Danny continually whispered to me that he had seen this one or that one. My pride knew no bounds.

Danny drew the "straight" kids like a magnet. He looked so happy, walked so tall, and had an air of complete self-confidence. Some of the druggies passed with, "Hey man, how's it goin'?" then scampered away like scared rabbits.

Tonight we went to the school for a ball game. The senior girls grabbed Danny and sang, "We're glad to see you, Danny."

Oct. 29: We went to an ice-cream supper. A senior boy came up to Danny, twice, asking how he could get what Danny had. Danny shared his feelings with him. Then he and his buddy climbed ropes, played volleyball, and enjoyed themselves.

Was so wonderful not to have to worry about my straight son. The last ice-cream social I attended I had attended with Jon during my separation from Ken. Danny had come in for a minute—then split.

The three-day leave passed in a round of happy memories. Although Danny met several druggie "friends" during the weekend, he told each one that it wasn't in his best interest to continue the friendships.

The drive back to Atlanta seemed much longer than usual. I fought inwardly with myself. Danny seemed so responsive, so loving, so all-together that I secretly longed to have him stay home. Realistically, though, I knew many challenges still faced him with his program in Atlanta.

The next month brought him into the fifth phase of his program.

Nov. 18: We stood in Open Meeting. My voice choked-

up as I told Danny how proud I felt that he'd made fifth phase. Ken told him what a fine young man he had become.

Nov. 21: Danny got angry as he tried to get several things done in preparation for school and responsibilities at the [Straight] building. When he dialed the phone I saw him cussing under his breath.

He left with a hasty goodbye. I felt a lot of hurt. When we picked him up from school, he made amends first thing. Said he didn't start feeling better until fourth period when he called and talked with a staff dad.

Ken and I progressed in our program, also. Constantly working on my enabling habits, I found it hard to shed the old skin of continually trying to lead my family's lives for them. Several times each day I fought the urge to "enable" a family member.

Picking up my MI notebook, I worked my problem out on paper. Slowly a peace emerged inside like a rainbow after a thunderstorm as I again realized my powerlessness.

I choose to worry about Ken's mood swings even though I am sensitive to them. It makes me uptight and I pass this feeling on to others. I don't like feeling uptight and tense. If I don't change this tenseness, I fear that I might crack under it. Therefore, if I refuse to take the responsibility for his actions, I can relax more. That will help me give more attention to my own feelings. Since I know I cannot change his attitude, I must turn my problem over to God.

Good Points: I enjoy giving of my feelings to others. I like sharing my experiences with others and am glad when I can actually help them.

Goals: I'm going to seek to get in touch with my own feelings about Ken's mood swings. Then I will be able to express to him the frustration his moods create in me.

Blessings: Getting to have a good day of shopping with Anita. We laughed a lot and I enjoyed the relaxation.

Many days I wrote more than one MI. Cushioning me

like a featherbed of peace, they showed me in black and white my powerlessness. Also they reminded me that only God could bring order into my life, only He could change my family members. Only God could give me serenity.

Peace slowly flowed into our family like gentle waves washing over a sand castle. Weekends at Atlanta became a family fun-time as we visited amusement parks, rode, laughed, and talked. Sometimes we went on picnics to small parks where Danny and Jon enjoyed the play ground swings, climbed monkey bars, and slid down the slides together.

Danny's maturation had stopped when he began doing drugs. Eventually it lagged several years behind his 17 years. The years when he should have enjoyed being an early-teen, he spent involved in fighting back emotions that he could not handle because of his drug use. Now he needed to catch up with his age.

It always brought a fresh excitement to me to be with him. Often he was like opening a new book for the first time. *He wants to be with us,* I thought to myself. *My son doesn't mind if I put my arm around him. In turn he shows me attention and affection, is so kind to Jon, and now puts his arm around his father.*

Jon lived for the trips to see Danny. "My big brother can do 50 pushups. My big brother is so much fun. How much longer 'til we go to Atlanta, Mom?"

The homes Danny stayed in seemed to be just the environment he needed. Most of them were Christian-oriented. Many times he curled up on a makeshift sleeping bag on the floor with Jon when we spent the night with the host parents.

One evening Jon had slept alone while Danny carried on other responsibilities with a newcomer. Returning from the rest room, Ken bumped an antique sewing machine head mounted on a shelf just over where Jon slept.

I awoke to the noise of the machine crashing to the

floor, shelf and all. But my husband's sobs frightened me more. Cradling his youngest son in his arms, he kept repeating, "I've killed him. I've killed him!"

Danny and the host parents came running. When the lights flashed on, a very confused Jon sat rubbing his eyes. He didn't have a scratch on him although the machine lay not six inches from his pillow. Ken's relief brought tears to all our eyes.

"God gave him back to me," he whispered as we settled down once more. "I'll have to remember that always."

Five hours driving to Atlanta, staying up past midnight each night, rising early to help with the responsibilities in the parent home, mountains of wash, mountains of food, and boys everywhere. I thrived on it and could scarcely wait until the next visit.

As I watched other mothers being strong with their children, it gave me new strength. Listening as other parents discussed various problems, I heard parents giving firm, tough love regardless of how the child received it.

Gradually I realized that I could say how I felt, even though the person might not accept it with open arms. Now I knew that my mental health depended on me being vulnerable regardless of the consequences. I must not stuff down my feelings to protect myself or anyone else.

"Ken, I feel distant when you won't tell me what you're thinking."

"Do ya think ya have to know everything?"

"No, do you think I want to know everything?"

"You're always butting into other people's business."

"I butt into other people's business?"

"Yeah, you always have to ask David about his personal life. You have to check up on Anita and Randy like they were children. They can take care of themselves, ya know."

"So, I'm not treating them as adults?"

"You bet you aren't. You're so busy taking care of them, you don't even notice me."

"You would like me to spend more time with you?"

"Yeah, this last week you've been doing something every night."

"Well, shall we go out to dinner tonight?"

God would transform Ken in His own time, as my husband felt willing. I could change only me and in doing so, I found Ken easier to get along with.

I felt a special love for the road leading to the Straight facilities, a fact that I mentioned to my family every trip. "I could just kiss this road. I love coming here."

"You wouldn't if you had to come every day," Danny commented.

"You wouldn't if you had to drive it all the time," Ken added.

But I knew why I loved it so. Here at this building I found the person in me, the enthusiastic individual who had stood as president of my high school class, the perceptive person who knew when someone felt discouraged, and the religious person who had discovered how to let go and allow God to take care of others in His time.

My son was nearing the end of his program. He looked like a winner and was—a daily winner over the drugs his life had been chained to for three years.

Dec. 5: Danny made trainee. [That meant that he would assist in the Straight program.] He sounded so happy and proud on the phone. Now he helps lead out in group, tries to take care of parent problems, or passes them on to someone who can.

Dec. 19: Today we brought Danny home for Christmas leave. When we drove by school, we met David. As we talked a few minutes, David seemed nervous—Danny quiet. After David left, Danny cried. He said he'd felt so weak and scared. I felt torn up inside and prayed that God would lead them both.

Dec. 21: Danny went to the school and saw some of the

kids. He said he felt better and less scared. Also he talked to David again.

Dec. 22: I came home after Jon's Christmas party at school. The roads were icy. We enjoyed being cozy at home.

Dec. 23: I stayed home today. David stopped by about 4:30. He and Danny shared some, though Danny is uncomfortable around him. We talked as the fire burned in the fireplace—even Dad. We discussed Dad's changes and Danny's changes.

Anita and Randy arrived about 8:00. We all had a good time seeing our new grandson, Nicholas. He is so sweet and such a bright baby. It's fun being a grandma.

Dec. 24: We were all together in church. The most special day in so many years! David came home to lunch with us. We ate spaghetti (the boys' favorite), then walked to Nana and Papa's in zero weather.

Later all the in-laws came to our house. They were all so proud of Danny. I could tell he was very proud of himself.

Christmas: Our family had the best Christmas ever! Ken didn't make any scenes. Grandma and Grandpa came over to open gifts. We went up to Nana's. Rebecca and Leo visited.

As Danny sat on the floor with Jon, helping him put together a plastic car model, I snapped a photograph of them. Later they enjoyed operating Danny's remote control car that we had given him. They were as close as two sheets of paper.

Each day Danny has been home, a druggie friend has called or stopped by. Danny seems to handle it well. He tells them how good it feels to be straight and that he can't be their friend anymore.

Dec. 27: Danny went by to see the judge, and he's letting him get his license back early. Said he felt very proud of Danny's progress. Danny seemed so proud to talk to him.

Dec. 28: Danny and Ken went to get his license. He

drove the car back home and is so happy to be able to drive again.

David came over along with my friend Lois, her son Wayne, and her new husband. We had pizza. What a good time! God is so good and His name is greatly to be praised for His wonderful works among the children of men.

Dec. 29: Today I had to say goodbye to my sweet grandson, Anita, Randy, and my new son, Danny. How I love them all. Anita and Randy volunteered to take Danny back to Straight.

The next step for Danny was graduation. When he returned to Atlanta after Christmas, I knew it would be only a matter of days, thus I wasn't surprised when the phone rang one cold January day.

Jan. 17: A junior staff member called from Straight and said we should be at Open Meeting Friday night. When I asked him why, he said something big was going to happen. He explained that he couldn't say what, just be there.

Stunned with joy, I stood in the center of the kitchen for five minutes. I knew Danny had finished his program at Straight. Then I called Anita and they made arrangements to attend her brother's graduation.

Jan. 20: Came down yesterday to Atlanta. Danny seems confident he's 7-stepping [the final stage of the Straight program]. We spent all day trying to throw him off the track by making other plans for the weekend.

Secretly I ordered a cake with "Congratulations 7-Stepper" written on it. His foster parents and I tried hard not to act too excited as we hedged all questions from him.

When Danny finally left for school, I went to the store for crepe paper, punch, and the cake. The dining room looked beautiful decorated in streamers and balloons as we prepared it for a celebration party after Danny's graduation from the program. Jon made a huge sign saying, "Congratulations, Danny. We love you."

Anita and Randy made it about 15 minutes before the

Open Meeting. Parents began talking to the guys. The first ones said "Love you, group," instead of "Love you, daughter." The staff asked if they didn't have a daughter in the program. When they said Yes, the staff said, "Meet your new Straight daughter."

Then the man said he needed to make it even. "Danny, you're a 7-stepper." I knew my dream had come true. Three guys and three girls graduated. Each group of parents and loved ones stood with their graduate.

Jon stood with all the family as we grouped around Danny. "I'm proud to have a 7-step brother," he declared. Randy, visibly shaken, his six-foot-plus strong figure bowed with emotion, said, "Danny, you have certainly changed for the better since you stayed with Anita and me."

"I'm so happy to have such a neat brother. I love you, Danny." Anita welcomed a hug from him.

"Danny, you have made me very happy," I told him. "I enjoy having a teenage son I can relate to. I appreciate your new-found integrity." As his hazel eyes looked with clearness and honesty into mine, I realized God had given me a special privilege that night.

As Ken put his hand on his son's shoulder, clearing his throat, he paid no attention to the tears running down his cheeks. "Danny, I love you very much. I'm glad to have my son back. I appreciate the staff putting up with you so long."

Tears in his own eyes, my son took the microphone. "Thanks, Dad, for the good words. Your love means everything to me. Thanks, Mom, for standing by me so long. I love you. I love you Jon, Anita, and Randy."

Danny's decision to stay straight would be a daily one. And I must also admit daily and hourly my own powerlessness to protect him. A lifetime lay before him. The choice must always be his as to how he chose to spend it, whether he would abstain from drugs or not.

But we possessed new tools to handle our lives in a

growing way. While I could not control anyone else's choices, I could control my own.

God grant me the serenity to accept the things I cannot change, to change the things I can, and the wisdom to know the difference.

A BEGINNING

Epilogue

Drugs are a one-way street. No matter how much you think you can keep them under control, you can't. I know this. Since my treatment, I've had some real hard times and have fallen back to alcohol. Every time this has happened, though, it has done nothing but make the problems worse and resolved nothing. The only way to deal with life is action, not running away to a temporary high. Relapse may happen, but you cannot stay there or death is certain. I know. *I've been there.* You have to believe me.

Danny